A Strong Mind
in a Strong Body

New German-American Studies
Neue Deutsch-Amerikanische Studien

Don Heinrich Tolzmann
General Editor

Vol. 12

PETER LANG
New York • Washington, D.C./Baltimore • Boston
Bern • Frankfurt am Main • Berlin • Vienna • Paris

Dolores J. Hoyt

A Strong Mind in a Strong Body

Libraries in the German-American Turner Movement

PETER LANG
New York • Washington, D.C./Baltimore • Boston
Bern • Frankfurt am Main • Berlin • Vienna • Paris

Library of Congress Cataloging-in-Publication Data

Hoyt, Dolores J.
A strong mind in a strong body: libraries in the German-American
Turner movement / Dolores J. Hoyt.
p. cm. — (New German-American studies; v. 12)
Includes bibliographical references and index.
1. German Americans and libraries—History—19th century. 2. Cooperative
society libraries—United States—History—19th century. 3. German Americans—
Societies, etc.—History—19th century. 4. German Americans—Intellectual life.
I. Title. II. Series: New German-American studies; vol. 12.
Z711.8.H68   026'.00089'31073—DC20   96-31803
ISBN 0-8204-3348-9
ISSN 1043-5808

Die Deutsche Bibliothek-CIP-Einheitsaufnahme

Hoyt, Dolores J.:
A strong mind in a strong body: libraries in the German-American turner
movement / Dolores J. Hoyt. –New York; Washington, D.C./Baltimore;
Boston; Bern; Frankfurt am Main; Berlin; Vienna; Paris: Lang.
(New German-American studies; Vol. 12)
ISBN 0-8204-3348-9
NE: GT

The paper in this book meets the guidelines for permanence and durability
of the Committee on Production Guidelines for Book Longevity
of the Council of Library Resources.

Printed in the United States of America.

ACKNOWLEDGMENTS

Assistance and encouragement by Drs. David Kaser and Eberhard Reichmann throughout the original writing process is greatly appreciated. My gratitude also extends to the Indiana University Center on Philanthropy, at Indiana University-Purdue University, Indianapolis, for a Doctoral Fellowship which provided financial support for research on this work.

In addition, the many archivists who assisted me must be thanked, in particular: Monique Bourque of the Balch Institute for Ethnic Studies; Eric Pumroy of the Special Collections & Archives at the IUPUI University Libraries; Holly Hall of the Special Collections, Washington University Libraries; Judith A. Simonsen of the Milwaukee County Historical Society; Carol S. Verble of the Missouri Historical Society; Darla Gebhard of the Brown County Historical Museum. Some of these people have moved on to other institutions, but all are to be commended for their dedicated service to researchers. Also, Ray Gnat of the Indianapolis-Marion County Public Library and Jean Gosebrink of the St. Louis Public Library were of great assistance in identifying and providing access to resources for those institutions.

A special thank you is given to all the individual American Turner members who assisted with this project. I will not list them individually for fear of omitting someone, but their generosity and interest in my project was much appreciated.

This edition would not have been successfully completed without the able editorial and secretarial assistance of Allison Kopczynski, and the professional indexing of Mary Frisby, two gracious and supportive colleagues.

Finally, I would like to thank my husband, Giles, and son, Kip, for their patience, understanding, and encouragement.

TABLE OF CONTENTS

LIST OF ILLUSTRATIONS

LIST OF TABLES

LIST OF CHARTS

I

INTRODUCTION

Much of the library literature pertaining to early American library development ignores or minimizes library development and support for libraries within ethnic groups. The records of such groups are often not in English, frequently handwritten, and not generally accessible. The archives of the American Turners and some of its local Turner groups provide a unique opportunity to study primary materials related to an influential and large German-American organization. A close examination of the role of libraries in the American Turners movement provides an important case study for the role of libraries and reading in ethnic groups during a period of major immigration to the United States, 1850 to 1918.

Minutes, library catalogs, and remnants of collections of Turner organizations were examined, as well as statistical records of the National Federation. Comparisons of holdings were made among Turner libraries and against the German-language collections of several major public libraries to ascertain the uniqueness of materials. This case study, when added to those of other ethnic groups, will form a revised national composite of early American library development.

Other than an article by Robert Cazden, "Libraries in the German-American Community and the Rise of the Public Library Movement,"[1] and isolated and scant information on private collections or reading societies buried within larger works on German-Americans, little is known about the place of reading and libraries within the German-American community. A systematic study of this area is missing from the library literature.

The tri-centennial celebration of German immigration to America in 1983 kindled a reexamination of the role of this ethnic group in the development of the United States. Two World Wars had previously made such studies unpopular. The general disillusionment with the melting pot theory of history has also contributed to the recent reevaluation of ethnic studies. The renewal of interest in one's German heritage has also resulted in the discovery of many primary materials which were previously unaccessible or unknown.

Case studies which examine the role of libraries and reading within individual German-American communities and societies are needed to provide a clearer national composite of library development in the United States. This study will deal with one such German-American society, the American Turners, whose motto, "a strong mind in a strong body," professed its commitment to an educated membership. Early bylaws (1854) of the American Turners indicated that each Turner organization should have a library for its members. This group was also chosen for this study because of its national scope and early establishment in 1850 and continuance throughout the major waves of German immigration. The American Turners were a German-American organization with the emphasis on American. One had to have American citizenship or have applied for citizenship to become a member of this society. Thus, this was a group which was dedicated to contributing to its new homeland. Since the strongest, overt influence of German-Americans on American society was pre-World War I, this study deals with the critical time period before 1918.

Background

German-Americans and libraries. Germans composed one of the major ethnic groups which immigrated to the United States. Dinnerstein reports from United States immigration statistics that the Germans were the single largest ethnic group entering between 1851 and 1890.[2] In addition, Germans are listed as the second largest ethnic origin group in 1971 census statistics (25,661,000) with the combined grouping of English, Scotch, and Welsh (31,006,000) being the first.[3] Although German immigration was not limited to any distinct time period, there were three periods of major influx, that of the 1850s following the Revolution of 1848, that of the 1870s during a period of economic and political unrest in Europe, and that of the early 1880s.

Generally, the Germans were eager to become "Americans" and to support a country in which they hoped to escape the ills that they had experienced in Europe. Initially, however, their language and culture isolated them from the Anglo-American establishment, causing them to join together for mutual support. In a sense, this "isolation" made the Germans "more German" than they might have been in their own homeland.[4] In addition, Germans did not generally band together with other ethnic groups in the United States. Dinnerstein characterizes the Germans as very clannish and maintaining "the most extensive number of [ethnic] newspapers, fraternal organizations, gymnastic and cultural societies, choral and athletic groups, and benevolent organizations."[5] What escapes Dinnerstein is that the numerically overwhelming presence of German-speaking immigrants in many areas was at the root of this ethno-linguistic cultural continuity that he and others label as being "clannish." In fact, Still's history of Milwaukee noted that by 1910 later immigrant groups were less integrated into society than the German-Americans.[6]

Some of the sources claim that the new German immigrant was "better educated and more widely read than their American counterparts ...,"[7] and that these recent arrivals felt that certain cultural amenities were lacking in their new communities.[8] However, the Germans did not see a contradiction in being American and maintaining their German heritage. They formed many organizational entities to support or maintain their cultural, political, and educational viewpoints such as singing societies, Free-Thinkers societies, German-English schools, and gymnastic societies. At the same time, they fought bravely as individuals and as German regiments in the Civil War or whenever called upon to defend their new country. One had to be an American citizen, or have applied for citizenship, to join the major German gymnastic group, the American Turners. Assimilation was desired by the Germans, but not at the expense of the complete abandonment of their cultural and linguistic heritage.[9]

Although a number of sources refer to many of the German immigrants as being from the intellectual class, particularly those leaving after the Revolution of 1848, little mention is made of their involvement with reading and the development of libraries in America. Most information about the association of this ethnic group with libraries is contained in isolated statements referring to specific libraries, donations, or contributions of a given individual in general histories of German-Americans or German-Americans in specific states. Robert Cazden is the major, or even sole, researcher who has concentrated on this connection in the literature on libraries.[10] Cazden has also contributed other works related to this area such as that on the German-American press, including the impressive work, *A Social History of the German Book Trade in America to the Civil War.*[11]

In the publication, *Milestones to the Present: Pages from the Library History Seminar V,*[12] several articles referred to states with strong German immigrant populations. Little mention was made of German contributions to the development of libraries or the support of reading. Donald Davis' article on Texas quoted a source which referred to German reading rooms established before 1876, even though only six social libraries were listed in the 1876 report on libraries:

> German reading rooms thrived in Galveston and San Antonio at mid-century [1850s]; the San Antonio room boasted 1,400 volumes.[13]

However, that is the extent to which German-American involvement was mentioned in this article.

In this same collection, John Colson's article on library development in Wisconsin claimed that the New England migrant was the main impetus to library development there. Colson further stated that the German-American population did not contribute to early library development in any significant way, even though Germans represented one-third of the population in Milwaukee alone. In the Young Men's Association, one of the major social libraries of Milwaukee, only 5% of the subscribers were German, nor did any German hold an office in this organization from 1847–1877. In contrast, he stated that there were New England migrants as officers of the predominantly German singing societies.[14] Although he did not discuss this phenomenon extensively in the article, he did mention that the New England migration came earlier and that the New Englanders quickly gained political control in Wisconsin.

The only article found which directly discussed the positive effect of the German-American community on library development was that by Robert Cazden in this same collection.[15]

The statistics that Cazden cited indicate the strong involvement of the German-American community in reading and education. He reported that before World War I, "over 5,000 German-language newspapers and periodicals are listed in the standard bibliography," and "a directory published in 1888 listed 185 [German-language book] outlets in 208 cities spread over 32 states." Also, Cazden stated that many "libraries whose main function was to supply German-language reading matter" were founded, often in connection with some type of German educational group.[16] He continued by citing examples of support for free public libraries by the German-American communities, and of German representation on the Board of Directors of many public libraries, including such cities as Milwaukee, Sheboygan, New York, and St. Louis.[17] Some private or social German-American libraries were turned over to, or even became the nucleus of, public library collections, as was the case in Peoria, Illinois (2,000 volumes in 1881) and Belleville, Ohio (9,000 volumes).[18]

Thus, Cazden's article, by necessity of its brevity, skimmed the surface of the German-American community's involvement in reading and library development and seemingly contradicted Colson's statements in the same collection.

Studies such as Cazden's *A Social History of the German Book Trade in America to the Civil War*, noted above, Knoche's *The German Immigrant Press in Milwaukee*[19] and Dolmetsch's *The German Press of the Shenandoah Valley*,[20] showed the scope of the German-American press activity within the United States for this early period. David Kaser's work on reading in Civil War camps also documented the availability of the German-American press to the Civil War German-speaking soldier.[21] One example of the level of readership in the German-American community is *Frank Leslie's Illustrirte Zeitung* (founded in 1857), an illustrated weekly, which had a circulation of 41,000 in 1873.[22] Such studies show the extent of the pre-World War I German-American press and the obvious readership to support such publications.

Turners and libraries. Literature related to the nineteenth-century German background of the American Turners provides an understanding of the political, economic, and social scene from which the Turner membership immigrated. Since each ethnic group came laden with its own cultural background, it is natural that this background would color its expectations and interactions with the new homeland. A brief review of educational and political background is provided by such works as Reinhardt's *Germany: 2000 Years*,[23] and Treitschke's contemporary view, *History of Germany in the Nineteenth Century*.[24] McClelland's *State, Society, and University in Germany, 1700–1914*[25] yields valuable information on the enormous effect of the university community in the everyday life of this time period. It is from this nineteenth-century, German university environment that the political reform activities of the Turners first emanated. McClelland's work greatly enhances the understanding of this movement's pervasive effect within the total society. Several works define the role of libraries and reading in nineteenth-century Germany. Peter Gradenwitz' article, "Books and Reading in Germany 200 Years Ago,"[26] relates the availability and types of literature available to the German public. Ladislaus Buzas' extensive work, *German Library History, 800–1945*,[27] provides insight into the type and nature of library development extant for this time period. While scholarly libraries had a strong tradition in German-speaking lands, public library development was limited prior to the 1850s.[28] Public library development in Germany paralleled political reform, supported by the Turners, which recognized the power of education to better the lives of the lower economic classes.

General literature concerning the German immigrant community in the United States prior to World War I, particularly in relation to its intellectual aspects, provides a framework in which the German-American Turner organizations can be placed. This literature includes such works as Albert Faust's *The German Element in the United States with Special Reference to it Political, Moral, Social, and Educational Influence*,[29] Gustav Körner's *Das Deutsche Element in den Vereinigten Staaten von Nordamerika, 1818–1848*,[30] Victor

Wolfgang von Hagen's *The Germanic People in America*,[31] and Trommler and McVeigh's *America and the Germans*.[32] Indeed, Körner profiles many famous German-American Turners in his work.

There are a number of useful background works on German-Americans in various states or cities. One group of these was authored by nineteenth-century contemporaries such as Theodore Stempfel, *Fünfzig Jahre unermüdlichen deutschen Strebens in Indianapolis*,[33] and Wilhelm Hense-Jensen, *Wisconsin's Deutsch-Amerikaner bis zum Schluß des neunzehnten Jahrhunderts*.[34] Another group of histories includes such later scholarly treatments as Lich's *The German Texans*,[35] Holmquist's *They Chose Minnesota: A Survey of the State's Ethnic Groups*,[36] Glasrud's *A Heritage Fulfilled: German-Americans (Die Erfüllte Herkunft)*,[37] Zeitlin's *Germans in Wisconsin*, Giles Hoyt's "Germans" in *Peopling Indiana: The Ethnic Experience*,[39] and Probst's *The Germans in Indianapolis, 1840–1918*.[40] The German-American histories not only provide general background on German-American communities, but also serve as a source for specifics about local Turners or libraries and reading. There are numerous smaller publications about German-Americans in state histories, but few are related to German-American Turner societies.

Contemporary articles in the library literature from 1850 to 1920 are of limited help in trying to establish the contribution of foreigners to library development, but they set the tone for the contemporary library community's concept of service to the foreign-born. Library literature cited in the *Bibliography of Library Economy*[41] under the heading "Library and the foreign population," for the period 1894 to 1915, concentrated on service to the immigrant population (63 articles). In the period from 1916 to 1920, the tone changed from one of the library helping to Americanize the foreigner. The United States Bureau of Education 1875 survey, *Public Libraries in the United States of America*[42] is invaluable in its presentation of statistics for many types of libraries, including Turner libraries. The historical essays on libraries in individual cities also contribute much to the understanding of library development as viewed by nineteenth-century library historians.

Literature related to the American Turners is not extensive. Barney's historiography of the German-American Turnverein movement[43] confirms this fact, although he has omitted a few works of significance such as Binz' *Gymnastic Societies in St. Louis, 1850–1913*,[44] and Wagner's "Turner Societies and the Socialist Tradition."[45] These exemplify the difficulty of uncovering some of these sources, many of which have been prepared as Masters theses. General histories of the Turners are few. H. Metzner's *History of the American Turners*[46] is in its fourth edition, recording major events and concepts of the American Turners. H. Ueberhorst's *Turner unterm Sternenbanner: Der Kampf der deutsch-amerikanischen Turner für Einheit, Freiheit und soziale Gerechtigkeit 1848 bis 1918*[47] provides a review of the origin of the Turner movement in Germany and an overview of the American Turner movement, including background information on some of the German-Americans important in the early years of the American Turners. C. E. Miller's *Der Turner Soldat*[48] describes the role of the Turner soldier in the Civil War.

Information about the American Turners is also available in several publications on the Forty-Eighters, many of whom were Turners. This category of literature includes such titles as Carl Wittke's *Refugees of Revolution: The German Forty-Eighters in America*[49] and Brancaforte's *The German Forty-Eighters in the United States*.[50]

Relatively little is available about individual Turner societies or Turners in a specific city. A number of such publications were written by Turners in celebration of anniversaries. Generally such histories are pamphlets without references to sources of information. A number of these anniversary histories are available in the Indiana University-Purdue Univeristy Indianapolis (IUPUI) Special Collections and Archives. One such example is the Indianapolis Turnverein anniversary pamphlet, *Seventy-Fifth Anniversary 1851–1926*.[51] Several minor journal articles were found to be anecdotal in nature. A more substantial work is Stempfel's *Fünfzig Jahre unermüdlichen deutschen Strebens in Indianapolis*,[52] which not only gives the history of Germans in Indianapolis, but also emphasizes the Turners. R. Binz' "Gymnastic Societies in St. Louis 1850–1913"[53] treats the many Turner organizations in St. Louis. Katja Rampelmann's "Small Town Germans: The Germans of Lawrence, Kansas, from 1854 to 1918"[54] deals extensively with the Turner organization in that community. Rampelmann's work treats libraries to the extent that she includes an appendix listing the works in the Lawrence Turnverein library based on the surviving volumes. Walter Osten, a Milwaukee Turner, describes to his fellow Turners the nature of the Milwaukee Turnverein library, given to the Milwaukee County Historical Society, in two articles published in the *Milwaukee Turner*.[55] The latter was the only source found dealing primarily with the nature of Turner libraries.

A significant major work which identifies sources of primary materials is the *Research Guide to the Turner Movement in the United States* by Eric Pumroy and Katja Rampelmann.[56] Many of these materials identified remain in private hands. This excellent work also includes invaluable historical information on these societies.

As was mentioned above, there are many fine sources of information on the German-American press and book trade in the United States, but little on the German-American community and libraries. The exploration of libraries within the American Turner organizations will fill this void for one segment of the multi-faceted German-American community.

Exploring Turner Libraries

This exploration of Turner libraries will: 1) examine the attitude and directives of the national federation of American Turners relating to libraries from 1850 to 1918; 2) determine the extent to which the local Turner organizations carried out the national directives regarding libraries; 3) determine what local circumstances influenced Turner library development; 4) compare the characteristics of American Turner libraries to other community libraries containing German-language materials.

To achieve these ojbectives, the following questions will be addressed in this study: 1) What was the stated role of libraries in the national German-American association, the American Turners? 2) Does the evidence support the proposition that the stated role was achieved? 3) Were all local American Turner libraries similar in nature? 4) Did the community in which the individual Turner society was located and that community's library resources affect the nature of the Turner library collection? 5) How do the Turner library collections compare to other library collections of this same time period? 6) To what extent were these libraries used by the Turners and what type of material was read?

To begin, one method for categorizing the classes of German-American social and society libraries has been identified by Robert Cazden:

> 1) Social organizations for well-to-do Germans with interest in cultural
> and benevolent activities; 2) special interest groups such as singing,
> literary or library societies; 3) rationalist and freethought organizations
> like the independent congregations (*Freie Gemeinde*) and Free Men
> Societies founded by radical Forty-eighters; 4) the politically radical
> Turners (gymnastic societies); workingmen's groups including Wilhelm
> Weitling's *Arbeiterbund* branches, German labor unions, workers'
> educational societies and socialist organizations.[57]

To these classes could be added that of parochial or independent German schools.

This research deals with the fourth category, that of the American Turner organization which initially and during most of the period under investigation was considered politically radical. This group does not necessarily typify German-American organizations, but investigation shows that members of the American Turners also interacted with or were members of all the other groups listed by Cazden. The Turners were interested in all aspects of life—social, political, cultural, and educational—since these were the elements that influenced the well-rounded, critical-thinking citizen. Many of the other groups listed often met in Turner halls. These Turner halls were frequently focal points for German-American community activities. And, even though the group as a whole may have been considered politically radical, the American Turners represented a wide spectrum of political thought, from the more conservative to the very radical. Thus, a study of the role of libraries in the American Turner organizations may serve as one useful barometer of the role of libraries in the German-American community. The exception might be the German parochial community which set up many parallel structures to the moralistic, but generally anti-clerical, Turners.

The overview of the role of libraries in the American Turner organizations deals with the Turners at the national level. Statistics covering many categories of Turner organizational characteristics, including the number of library holdings, were available from 1866 to the present at the IUPUI Special Collections and Archives. These figures were analyzed to determine to what extent the local organizations followed the national directive to maintain libraries. More about the specific procedures used are given in Chapter II. Minutes of the national organization from 1854 were also examined.

The large number of local Turner organizations required some limitation for a manageable project. Specific groups in the Midwest were targeted because the Midwestern region contained many of the larger Turner libraries, cities with sizeable German-American communities, and known primary resources, and commanded the national headquarters for the American Turners for many years. Most primary resources were handwritten German documents, some of which were only available through private sources.

The administration of individual Turner libraries was determined by examining local constitutions and bylaws, bookplates containing library regulations, and information in minutes of the organizations.

The content of libraries was obtained through the location of some library remnants and catalogs. These collections were divided into subject categories similar to those used by Turner catalogs themselves. These categories are fully defined in the chapter on content. Content of contemporary catalogs from

German-language collections of several public libraries in the same cities as major Turner organizations were examined to determine the uniqueness of the Turner library materials.

The use of library collections included a significant primary resource outside the primary focus of the Midwestern region, that of the "Library Borrowers' Record" from the Wilmington, Delaware, Turngemeinde. This was the only such loan record which could be found and provided invaluable information of actual use patterns. Other primary sources included the minutes from the library committee of the New Ulm, Minnesota, Turnverein and from minutes of Turner organizations. Secondary resources were relied upon for supporting evidence of use in several cases. In two instances, some information was obtained through interviews with Turners.

The part of this study focusing on local Turner organizations includes those in New Ulm, Minneapolis, St. Paul, Milwaukee, Chicago, Indianapolis, Cincinnati, and St. Louis. These cities contained multiple Turner societies of varying size and dates of establishment. Organizations in Lawrence, Kansas, Louisville, Kentucky, and Wilmington, Delaware were only partially treated. More specific information on procedures are included within the appropriate chapters.

While evidence reveals that there is some commonality exhibited among Turner libraries, it is also clear that each community produced its own unique characteristics. Also, it is important to remember that the Turners represent only one segment of German-American society.

NOTES

[1]Robert E. Cazden, "Libraries in the German-American Community and the Rise of the Public Library Movement," in *Milestones to the Present*, ed. Harold Goldstein (Syracuse, N.Y.: Gaylord, 1978), 193–211.

[2]Leonard Dinnerstein and David M. Reimers, *Ethnic Americans: a History of Immigration and Assimilation* (New York: Dodd, Mead, 1975), 163–4.

[3]Ibid., 175.

[4]Glen E. Lich, *The German Texans* (San Antonio, TX: University of Texas, Institute of Texan Cultures, 1981), 83.

[5]Dinnerstein, 34.

[6]Bayrd Still, *Milwaukee: The History of a City* (Madison, WI: State Historical Society of Wisconsin, 1965), 278.

[7]Lich, 81.

[8]George T. Probst, "The Germans in Indianapolis, 1850–1914" (M.A. thesis, Indiana University, 1951); George T. Probst, *The Germans in Indianapolis, 1840–1918*, Rev. & illustrated ed., Eberhard Reichmann (Indianapolis, IN: German-American Center & Indiana German Heritage Society, 1989), 4. Probst refers to a letter (1836) by Jacob Schramm to his relatives in Germany stating his dislike of the "more primitive features of the new country."

[9]Lich, 137. A German immigrant and poet complains that the price of assimilation into the mainstream of American life was "too high; the Germans, according to him, gave up their most intimate possession, their mother tongue."

[10]Robert E. Cazden, "Libraries in the German-American Community," 193–211.

[11]Robert E. Cazden, *A Social History of the German Book Trade in America to the Civil War*, Studies in German Literature, Linguistics, and Culture, vol. 1, (Columbia, SC: Camden House, 1984).

[12]Harold Goldstein, ed., *Milestones to the Present: Papers from the Library History Seminar V*, (Syracuse, NY: Gaylord, 1978).

[13]Donald G. Davis, "The Rise of the Public Library in Texas," in *Milestones to the Present*, ed. Harold Goldstein (Syracuse, NY: Gaylord, 1978), 169.

[14]John C. Colson, "The Rise of the Public Library in Wisconsin: 1850–1920," in *Milestones to the Present*, ed. Harold Goldstein (Syracuse, NY: Gaylord, 1978), 185.

[15]Robert E. Cazden, "Libraries in the German-American Community," 193–211.

[16]Ibid., 196.

[17]Ibid., 203.

[18]Ibid, 203–4.

[19]Carl H. Knoche, *The German Immigrant Press in Milwaukee*, American Ethnic Groups: The European Heritage (New York: Arno, 1980).

[20]Christopher L. Dolmetsch, *The German Press of the Shenandoah Valley*, Studies in German Literature, Linguistics, and Culture, vol. 4 (Columbia, SC: Camden House, 1984).

[21]David Kaser, *Books and Libraries in Camp and Battle: The Civil War Experience*, Contributions in Librarianship and Information Science, no. 48 (Westport, CT: Greenwood Press, 1984).

[22]Christina Degina and Christiana Harzig, eds., *Deutschland im Gepäck* (Bremerhaven: Wirtschaftsverlag NW, 1987), [4].

[23]Reinhardt, Kurt F., *Germany: 2000 Years*, Vol. 2, *The Second Empire and the Weimar Republic* (New York: Ungar, 1961).

[24]Heinrich von Treitschke, *History of Germany in the Nineteenth Century*, Selections from the tr. of Eden and Cedar Paul, ed. & introd. Gordon A. Craig (Chicago: University of Chicago Press, 1974).

[25]Charles E. McClelland, *State, Society, and University in Germany, 1700–1914* (Cambridge: Cambridge University Press, 1980).

[26]Peter Gradenwitz, "Books and Reading in Germany 200 Years Ago," *AB Bookman's Weekly*, 8, no. 10 (7 Sept. 1987): 797-9.

[27]Ladislaus Buzas, *German Library History, 800–1945*, tr. William D. Boyd (Jefferson, NC: McFarland, 1986).

[28]Ibid., 360, 366–69.

[29]Albert B. Faust, *The German Element in the United States with Special Reference to its Political, Moral, Social, and Educational Influence*, 2 vols. (Boston: Houghton Mifflin, 1909).

[30]Gustav Phillip Körner, *Das Deutsche Element in den Vereinigten Staaten von Nordamerika, 1818–1848* (Cincinnati: Wilde, 1880; reprint, ed. Patricia A. Herminghouse, New York: P. Lang, 1986).

[31]Victor Wolfgang von Hagen, *The Germanic People in America* (Norman, OK: University of Oklahoma Press, 1976).

[32]Frank Trommler and Joseph McVeigh, eds., *America and the Germans: an Assessment of a Three-Hundred-Year History*, 2 vols. (Philadelphia, PA: University of Pennsylvania Press, 1985).

[33]Theodore Stempfel, *Fünfzig Jahre unermüdlichen deutschen Strebens in Indianapolis* (Indianapolis: Pitts & Smith, 1898); Theodore Stempel, *Fünfzig Jahre unermüdlichen deutschen Strebens in Indianapolis*, German/English ed. Giles R. Hoyt et al. (Indianapolis, IN: German-American Center & Indiana German Heritage Society, 1991).

[34]Wilhelm Hense-Jensen, *Wisconsin's Deutsch-Amerikaner bis zum Schluß des neunzehten Jahrhunderts*, 2 vols. (Milwaukee: Im Verlage der Deutschen Gesellschaft, Der Germania, 1900–02).

[35]Lich, op. cit.

[36]June Drenning Holmquist, ed., *They Chose Minnesota: A Survey of the State's Ethnic Groups* (St. Paul: Minnesota Historical Society Press, 1981).

[37]Clarence A. Glasrud, ed., *A Heritage Fulfilled: German-Americans (Die Erfüllte Herkunft)* (Moorhead, MN: Concordia College, 1984).

[38]Richard H. Zeitlin, *Germans in Wisconsin* (Madison: State Historical Society of Wisconsin, 1977).

[39]Giles Hoyt, "Germans," in *Peopling Indiana: The Ethnic Experience*, ed. Robert M. Taylor and Connie K. McBirney (Indianapolis, IN: Indiana Historical Society, 1966), 146-81.

[40]George T. Probst, "The Germans in Indianpolis."

[41]H. G. T. Cannons, *Bibliography of Library Economy: A Classified Index to the Professional Periodical Literature in the English Language Relating to Library Economy, Printing, Methods of Publishing, Copyright, Bibliography, Etc., from 1876 to 1920*, Reprint of the 1927 ed. (New York: B. Franklin, 1970).

[42]U.S. Bureau of Education. *Public Libraries in the United States of America: Their History, Condition, and Management: Special Report* (Washington, DC: GPO, 1876; Totowa, NJ: Rowman & Littlefield, 1971).

[43]Robert K. Barney, "The German-American Turnverein Movement: Its Historiography," in *Turnen und Sport: The Cross Cultural Exchange*, ed. Roland Naul, German and American Studies in Sport, vol. 1 (Münster, New York: Waxmann, 1991), 3-19.

[44]Roland Binz, "Gymnastic Societies in St. Louis, 1850-1913" (Master thesis, Washington University, St. Louis, MO, 1983).

[45]Ralf Wagner, "Turner Societies and the Socialist Tradition," in *German Workers' Culture in the United States, 1850 to 1920*, ed. Harmut Keil (Washington, DC: Smithsonian Institution Press, 1988), 221-39.

[46]Henry Metzner, *History of the American Turners*, 4th rev. ed. (Louisville, KY: National Council of the American Turners, 1989); Henry Metzner, *A Brief History of the American Turnerbund*, Rev. ed., tr. by Theodore Stempfel (Pittsburgh, PA: National Executive Committee of the American Turnerbund, 1924). Earlier German eds. published under Heinrich Metzner.

[47]Horst Ueberhorst, *Turner unterm Sternenbanner: Der Kampf der deutsch-amerikanischen Turner für Einheit, Freiheit und soziale Gerechtigkeit 1848 bis 1918* (München: Heinz Moos Verlag, 1978).

[48]C. Eugene Miller and Forrest F. Steinlage, *Der Turner Soldat: A Turner Soldier in the Civil War; Germany to Antietam* (Louisville, KY: Calmar Publications, 1988).

[49]Carl Wittke, *Refugees of Revolution: The German Forty-Eighters in America* (Philadelphia: University of Pennsylvania Press, 1952).

[50]Charlotte L. Brancaforte, ed., *The German Forty-Eighters in the United States*, German Life and Civilization, vol. 1 (New York: P. Lang, 1989).

[51]Indianapolis Socialer Turnverein, *Seventy-Fifth Anniversary 1851–1926* (n.p., n.d.).

[52]Stempfel, *Fünzig Jahre unermüdlichen deutschen Strebens in Indianapolis*.

[53]Binz, "Gymnastics Societies in St. Louis."

[54]Katja Rampelmann, "Small Town Germans: The Germans of Lawrence, Kansas, from 1854 to 1918," (M.A. thesis, University of Kansas, Lawrence, KS, 1993).

[55]Walter Osten, "The Milwaukee Turner Library," *The Milwaukee Turner* 6, no. 5 (May 1945): 1, 8; Walter Osten, "Turner Library Favors Early American History," *The Milwaukee Turner* 6, no. 7 (July 1945): 1, 4.

[56]Eric Pumroy and Katja Rampelmann, *Research Guide to theTurner Movement in the United States* (Westport, CT: Greenwood Press, 1996).

[57]Cazden, "Libraries in the German-American Community," 200.

II

OVERVIEW OF THE AMERICAN TURNER ORGANIZATIONS AND LIBRARIES

Role of Libraries as Defined by the National Federation of American Turners

The early leaders of the Turner societies were often those associated with the Forty-Eighters who left Germany after the unsuccessful Revolution of 1848. These leaders were in general more educated and convinced of the power of the written word. The participants of the Revolution of 1848 were strongly influenced by the academic world. As McClelland stated: "More than that of any other country in the world, Germany's liberal tradition came to be closely associated with the names of men who were professors in regular life."[1] In addition, McClelland noted that "[j]ust as educated and propertied classes in Germany were willing to vote professors into office, when possible, they were willing to subscribe to journals and newspapers whose tone was academic."[2] The university students taking part in the reform movement were on the whole much more radical than the professors. In general, the academic community had a great influence on the reform movement resulting in the revolution. Thus, it is not surprising that access to political writings would be considered essential to promotion of the radical idealism of the Turners. Not every Forty-Eighter was a Turner, or *vice versa*. The commitment to "radical" reform varied within the Turner organizations, both German and German-American, as much as it did within the Forty-Eighters themselves. However, it was the better educated who often founded, or quickly assumed leadership of, many of the early American Turner societies. It was these same leaders who then represented their societies at the national level.

The minutes of the American Turners provided the official federation position on libraries in relation to achieving the goals of the Turner organizations.[3] The first mention of libraries was at the national convention of 12 September 1854, only four years after the formation of the national organization, then called *Socialistischer Turnverein*. The motion referred to in the following—made by Turner Kaufmann from New York—was passed:

> Turner Kaufmann made a motion that not only the National Headquarters but also each Turner society should establish a library. Especially,

books on welfare, outstanding classical German works and standard authors should be obtained. Carried as paragraph 10 [of Bylaws].[4]

By the next convention in 1855 it must have been recognized that such a demand on the finances of the newly formed societies was not always practical. The bylaws were altered to state:

> ... the Turner organizations should have libraries, though in the beginning they may not have many books. Each Turner should help in this undertaking.[5]

In this same year it was suggested that the *Vorort*, or national headquarters, should purchase books wholesale and sell them to the societies at cost "in order to financially facilitate the start of libraries. This was rejected as impractical."[6] The movement of the *Vorort* at least each second year to a new site was surely one of the reasons this was considered impractical. Also, it would have involved an investment at the national level with no certainty of reimbursement in terms of purchases from the local level. There had already been discussion about local societies not paying dues on time or not paying for the required subscriptions to the national organ, the *Turnzeitung*.[7]

The slightly revised wording about libraries in the "Bylaws" attached to the 1855 National Convention minutes read as follows:

> Paragraph 9: The Turner societies should have libraries even if only a few books are available in the beginning. Every Turner should help to contribute to it to the best of his ability.[8]

In these same "Bylaws" it was recommended that societies establish: technical schools "in order to achieve a more general education for all turners;" day schools for juniors "for the purpose of training them not only physically but also mentally;" and reading classes "to establish scientific and practical reading classes through the medium of the turnerpaper in order to further the mental advancement of all societies."[9] Libraries were obviously one part of a concerted effort to develop an informed, educated citizenry.

In the 1855/1856 "Report" of the *Vorort*, concern for education was again expressed:

> We should form educational institutions for the citizens and for all free thinking people. Educating our youth and continued education for adults should always remain the aim of the national organization.[10]

The "Minutes" of the 1857 National Convention in Detroit, Michigan, reflected the concern that not all the societies were responding constructively to the major goals of the Turners. It was bemoaned that in some instances theater productions seemed to be outweighing educational and physical fitness objectives.[11] It was stated that technical schools were "generally lacking in proper management and financing" and that day schools were "also slow in making headway" although "instructions in English, reading, writing, and arithmetic [were] fostered in many societies with great success."[12] No specific mention was made concerning library development, but it could easily be assumed that the same unevenness would be found for that endeavor.

The "Report" of the *Vorort* for 1857/1858 stated that nineteen societies out of sixty reported having libraries. Sixteen of the libraries reported holding a total of 4,319 volumes.[13] The "Statutes for the Socialist Turnerbund of North America," attached to the "Minutes" of the National Convention for 1858 stated that one of the rights of the *Vorort* should be:

> Paragraph 24, Number 10: To arrange: ... b) "For good European and American newspapers and suitable articles about bodily exercises and collecting of books for the sum of $200 ...[14]

These library resources would assist in the production of the national paper as well as service the *Vorort*.

The Turners were ever self-critical. At the tenth National Convention in Chicago the warning was issued:

> However, a proper balance must be established to do justice to both mental culture and physical culture, otherwise one or the other will suffer. Besides the bodily exercises, the effort must be made to cultivate the thought of improvement and all around education as the first big effort to gain respect and to obtain a commanding position in life.[15]

Intellectual acumen was not to be neglected. In these same minutes forty organizations reported having libraries with a total of 15,000 volumes.[16] Yet at the 1860 National Convention in Rochester, New York, there were only thirty libraries reported with 7,000 volumes,[17] despite an increase from 70 to 73 societies. The drop in volumes was probably more a function of the particular societies that held memberships rather than a loss of holdings, even though fires were a frequent occurrence in these years. Political in-fighting and financial problems of societies characterized the early years of the Turnerbund, causing great fluctuations in membership. Most Turner societies also went into hiatus during the Civil War since so many members joined the Union forces.

By the 1866 National Convention in St. Louis, Missouri, it was decided that the library of the *Vorort* should be sold "because it is of no use to the Bund."[18] Since the site of the *Vorort* continually shifted, and the local societies were to have had their own libraries, it was probably superfluous to have a national library. The total number of library books held by the individual Turner societies in 1866 was reported to be 12,112 volumes. Turner writings represented 258 of these volumes. The national federation also ordered works on *Turnen*, which were recommended by the Turn Teacher's Congress and then distributed them to the district offices.[19] A list of other works available from the *Vorort* was also given.[20] These titles ranged from sixteen copies of the Brockhaus *Conversation Lexikon* to single copies of a number of scientific works such as Meier's *Die Erde*. Some of these titles may have been ones from the national library.

Turners were also very concerned about the availability of school books that would support rational, free thinking. A listing of such books was given in 1868.[21] Cazden stated that "the *Turner-Schulbücher* published by Ernst Steiger [were] the best known graded series of nonsectarian textbooks."[22]

Although a national library for the *Vorort* was rejected, 1868 Convention members were concerned about providing the national *Turnlehrer Seminar* with library resources of its own instead of depending on the hosting Turner society.[23] The *Turnlehrer Seminar* moved from place to place until its permanent establishment in 1907 as the Normal College in Indianapolis. Founding of a sizable, permanent library collection for it would have been as difficult as has it had been for the *Vorort* to form a national library.

From time to time books were recommended for purchase by the societies, e.g., Ravenstein's *Volksturnbuch*, in both German and English.[24] Another list of books available from the *Vorort* included titles on *Turnen* as well as four titles by Samuel Ludvigh.[25] Concern for "mental culture" was not forgotten although nationally more emphasis was being put on the promotion of Turner methods of physical education in public schools. In 1870 the following resolution was passed:

> The Turner societies are requested to provide for mental culture for all
> their members as an educational measure, through recitals, lectures, and
> debates at least once a month, to which the public should obtain free
> admission.[26]

By the time of the 1874 "Platform and Statutes" no mention was made about libraries. Emphasis was put on working toward establishment of good German-English schools, mandatory public schooling, promotion of physical education and German language classes in public schools, and cultural events at Turner societies including monthly educational talks, lectures, and debates.[27] Later "Platforms and Statutes" were concerned more with the administrative procedures of the organization, but the 1894 and 1896 "Platforms" each contained one sentence about libraries: "Ferner empfehlen wir den einzelnen Vereinen die Anschaffung sachbezüglicher Werke für die Vereinsbibliotheken."[28] Thus, the national direction appeared to move from recommending general libraries of "good" literature and writings consistent with the Turner philosophy to recommending writings more specifically related to *Turnen*.

At the time of the move of the *Turnlehrer Seminar* to Indianapolis in 1907, the 1907/1908 *Jahresberichte* reported that one of the facilities that would be available to the Normal College was a *Bibliothek- und Lesezimmer*. A further description followed:

> Im Bibliothek- und Lesezimmer befinden sich massive, staubfreie Bücherschränke, in welchen die alte Seminar Bibliothek und die zahlreichen neuangeschafften Werke untergebracht sind.[29]

Despite the declining mention of libraries at the national conventions, statistics about library holdings were one of the few items requested consistently by the national headquarters throughout the period of this study. Eighty-one different categories of statistical information were requested from the local organizations during the years 1866 to 1920. The categories recorded varied considerably over time. The few consistent ones were: library volumes, number of members, number of active members, number who were United States citizens, number of fencers, number of singing group members, number of Turn teachers, and if the society owned its building. There is some indication of importance in the fact that "library volumes" was one of these eight categories recorded throughout this time period. The Turners seemed proud of this component of their societies. A number of other items were added to those consistently collected after 1878. These concerned questions about indebtedness and worth, *Zöglingsvereine*, Turner students, and *"geistige Versammlungen."*

American Turner Organizations, 1866–1873

A great deal of development in the number and spread of Turner societies occurred during the early years. The national statistical records from

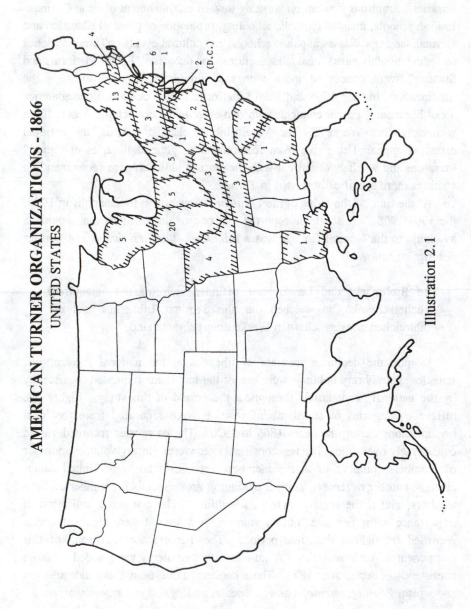

AMERICAN TURNER ORGANIZATIONS - 1866
UNITED STATES

Illustration 2.1

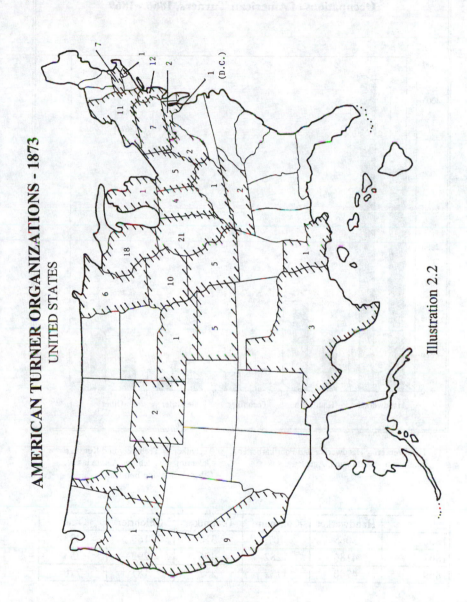

AMERICAN TURNER ORGANIZATIONS – 1873
UNITED STATES

Illustration 2.2

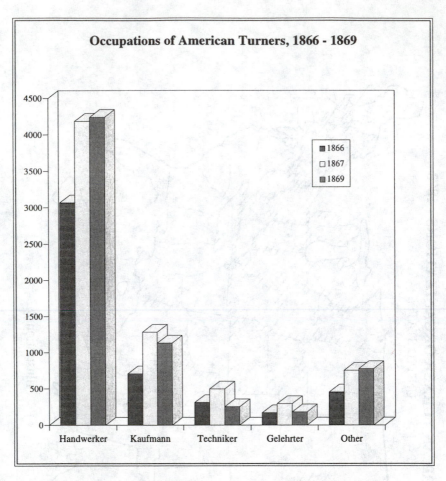

Occupations of American Turners, 1866 - 1869

Handwerker = Handwerker und Fabrikarbeiter   Techniker = Techniker und Kunstler
Kaufmann = Kaufmann, Agenten u.s.w.   Gelehrter = Gelehrter, Aerzte u.s.w.
                                              Other = Sonstige Berufsart

	Handwerker	Kaufmann	Techniker	Gelehrter	Other
1866	3065	707	310	169	453
1867	4186	1282	496	293	753
1869	4240	1132	252	181	776

Chart 2.1

1866–1873[30] provide an overview of this development. Illustrations 2.1 and 2.2 depict graphically the growth and geographical location by state of Turner societies which belonged to the federal organization for this period. The names of known Turner societies which did not belong to the federation were also occasionally listed, but they are not included here.

Turner societies were an urban phenomenon for the most part, although some of the urban communities on the frontier were small in comparison to the more developed eastern coast cities. Farmers, having toiled all day in the fields, had little need for a society to maintain their physical fitness, and they would have been less attracted to the radical philosophy espoused. Only during the 1866 to 1873 statistics were records kept of the occupations of Turner members. Chart 2.1 shows these occupations for the years 1866 to 1869. Ueberhorst found similar results when analyzing the occupations of the 795 members of the Pioneers who were founding members of Turner societies.[31] From 1870 to 1873 these figures were not systematically reported by the individual societies, and were therefore less meaningful.

The figures in Table 2.1 show the number of libraries and their relative sizes as reported for those years with fuller statistical data. Unfortunately, statistical reporting was uneven, and some societies did not provide data on libraries. Rather than assume that no library existed, these were recorded as "blank," for not recorded, instead of "zero," for no library.

Table 2.1 Relative Sizes of Turner Libraries, 1866 to 1873

Year	Size in Volumes	Number of Societies	% Of Total
1866	1000+	2	2.5%
	500–999	5	6.1%
	100–49	17	21.0%
	50–99	6	7.4%
	10–49	17	21.0%
	1–9	0	0.0%
	0	28	35.0%
	Blank	6	7.0%
Total		81	100.0%
1869	1000+	4	3.0%
	500–999	6	4.6%
	100–499	25	19.0%

Table 2.1 (cont.)

	50–99	8	6.1%
	10–49	21	16.0%
	1–9	6	4.6%
	0	47	35.9%
	Blank	14	11.0%
Total		**131**	**100.0%**
1872	1000+	8	4.5%
	500–999	6	3.4%
	100–499	34	19.1%
	50–99	20	11.2%
	10–49	29	16.3%
	1–9	5	2.8%
	0	0	0.0%
	Blank	76	42.7%
Total		**178**	**100.0%**
1873	1000+	4	2.9%
	500–999	9	6.5%
	100–499	29	20.9%
	50–99	23	16.6%
	10–49	24	17.3%
	1–9	8	5.8%
	0	0	0.0%
	Blank	42	30.2%
Total		**139**	**100.0%**

Although a strict comparison between years cannot be made because the reporting organizations varied, it is clear that over 50% of the societies did try to comply with the national directive to establish libraries, however small. This remains true even if the absence of a response is considered as meaning no library existed. The average of those libraries having over one hundred volumes is 28.4%. The following cities had societies with libraries numbering 1,000 volumes or more at some point during this time period (in descending order): Cincinnati, Ohio; Baltimore, Maryland; St. Louis, Missouri; Albany, New York; Milwaukee,

Wisconsin; New York City; Chicago, Illinois; Hamilton, Ohio. Five of these societies were located in the Midwest, the area which was chosen for more specific study for the years following.

Distribution of Turner Societies and Libraries in the Midwest

With the continued German immigration in the nineteenth century the number of Turner societies greatly increased. From 1866 to 1920 approximately 224 societies were identified for the Midwest alone. Since a sizable number of the larger libraries occurred in the Midwest, and the national headquarters of the American Turners were in the Midwest for a large part of the time under scrutiny, the focus of the study and the remaining statistical data analyzed will center on the Midwestern area. The federation of Turners was subdivided by regions or *Turnbezirke*. The geographical coverage of each *Turnbezirk* changed frequently throughout the years, depending on the total number of Turner members. In 1866 there were fourteen *Turnbezirke*, and in 1896 there were as many as thirty-three. By the early nineteen hundreds the number of *Turnbezirke* settled down to a steady twenty-four. The highest number of total library volumes reported for all Turner districts was 70,703 for 258 societies with a membership of 33,964 people in 1900. The highest membership, based on five-year increments, was 1895 with 39,870 members in 314 societies. If the total number of library volumes were divided by the membership, there were more books per member in 1880 than any successive year although that year had fewer books reported than any other. Libraries were not growing in proportion to the general membership.

The Turner regions, for which data from the national statistics from 1880 to 1920 were most closely analyzed, included Ohio, Central Illinois, Minnesota, Chicago, Wisconsin, St. Louis, and Indiana, sometimes with slight name changes. Northeastern Ohio was not included since this usually fell within a district called "Lake Erie." Likewise, the St. Louis *Turnbezirk* did not include all of Missouri. The *Turnbezirke* did include the primary Midwestern cities with major German-American populations such as Cincinnati, Indianapolis, Milwaukee, St. Louis, and Chicago. Minnesota was included because of the known primary materials available for New Ulm, Minnesota, a city which was developed primarily by Turners. In addition, data were recorded for every fifth year starting with 1880 because of the vast amount of material and because the data did not change markedly from year to year. Since the data for 1915 were not available in the resources consulted, the data for 1914 were substituted.

Illustrations 2.3, 2.4, and 2.5 show the number of Turner societies by state, or portion of a state, that belonged to the aforementioned *Turnbezirke* for the

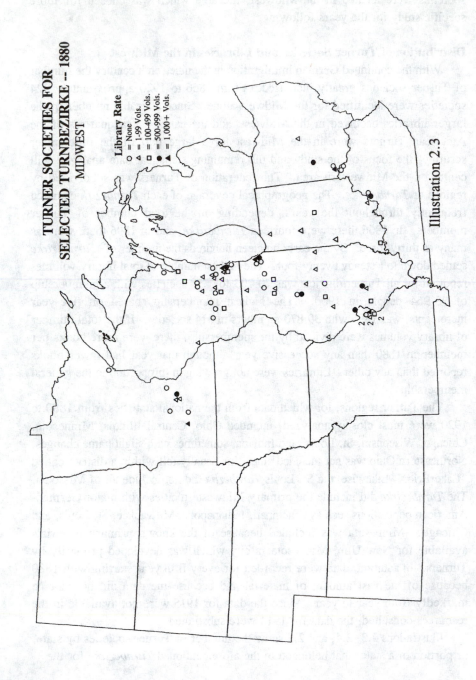

**TURNER SOCIETIES FOR
SELECTED TURNBEZIRKE -- 1880
MIDWEST**

Library Rate

○ = None
△ = 1-99 Vols.
□ = 100-499 Vols.
● = 500-999 Vols.
▲ = 1,000+ Vols.

Illustration 2.3

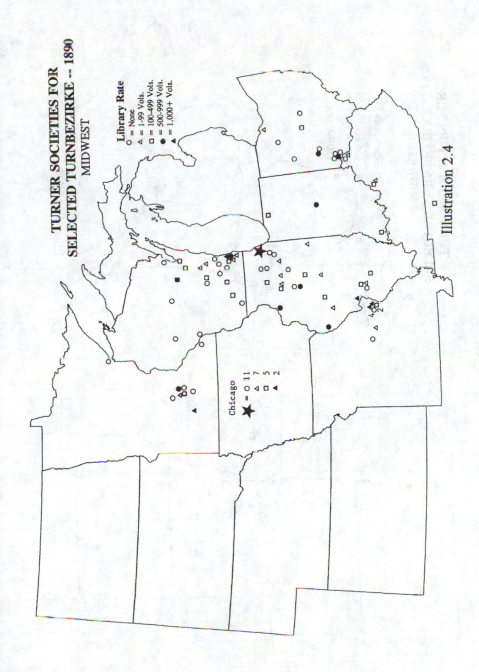

TURNER SOCIETIES FOR
SELECTED TURNBEZIRKE -- 1890
MIDWEST

Library Rate
○ = None
△ = 1-99 Vols.
□ = 100-499 Vols.
● = 500-999 Vols.
◄ = 1,000+ Vols.

Chicago
○ = 11
△ = 7
□ = 5
◄ = 2

Illustration 2.4

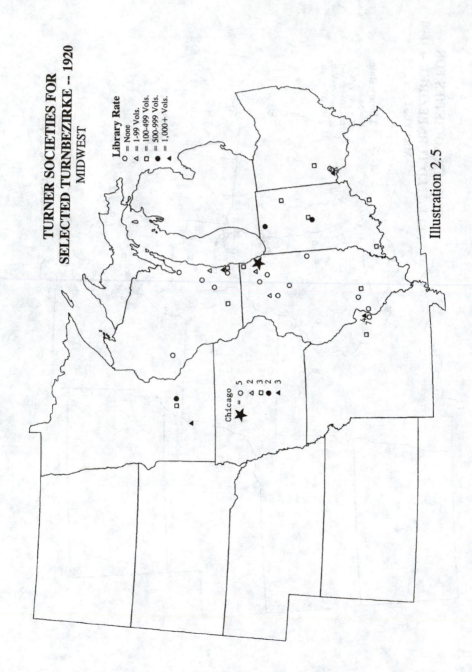

TURNER SOCIETIES FOR
SELECTED TURNBEZIRKE -- 1920
MIDWEST

Illustration 2.5

years 1880, 1890, and 1920 respectively. The 1890s represented the apex in the growth of Turner societies. Many societies were formed and disappeared between the years 1890 and 1920, and therefore are not represented on the illustrations. The decline in the numbers of societies from 1890 to 1920 is readily apparent. When viewed by percentage of societies in various library size categories, corresponding to those used above for 1866 to 1873, over half of all societies in a given year had at least some library holdings (see Table 2.2). The year 1910 was the one exception; 53.8% of the societies reported having no libraries that year. The percentage of libraries that held one thousand or more volumes increased from 6.5% in 1885 to 13.8% in 1920. However, the greatest percentage of all Turner libraries consistently held between 100 and 499 volumes.

The statistical data reported to the American Turners national headquarters were entered into a DBase program in two different sets. The first set was for all organizations from 1866 to 1873. This was kept separately since a number of categories were not used in later years and my interest was in discovering if there were any correlations with these specific categories which would not appear later. There were 666 observations in this data set. The second set of data was for the aforementioned Midwestern regions from 1880 to 1920, in five-year increments, and those parts of the 1866 to 1873 statistics which corresponded to those used in later years. There were 1,448 observations in this data set. Both data sets were then converted to a mainframe for manipulation by the SAS statistical program. A statistical expert was consulted to ensure the validity of statistical applications and procedures. Correlation analyses were run first in order to choose those items with a higher degree of correlation for the next processing step. There were so many categories for a multiple regression analysis that it was decided that a correlation analysis would assist in determining the most likely categories which should be used for the multiple regression analysis.

Since the reporting of Turner organizations was inconsistent, and since the categories shifted frequently, it was decided to run the analysis by year. The absence of data for a category dropped that observation from the analysis so a higher number of observations was obtained by year since the reporting within a given year for specific categories would naturally be higher. The resulting analysis indicated that for the earlier years of 1866 to 1872, the size of the organization was the greatest predictor of library size. It seems obvious that it would usually have taken a greater membership size to support financially the establishment of a new organization and a library. For the later years, 1873 to 1914, the age of the organization was the strongest predictor of library size. Those Turner societies founding sizeable libraries in their early development were also those most likely to maintain such a library in their later years.

AMERICAN TURNER LIBRARIES - MIDWESTERN REGION, 1880-1920

LIBRARY SIZE IN VOLUMES:

YEAR:	1,000+	% of Total	500-999	% of Total	100-499	% of Total	50-99	% of Total	10-49	% of Total	1-9	% of Total	0	% of Total	TOTAL
1880	5	6.5%	7	9.1%	15	13.0%	10	13.0%	13	16.9%	2	2.6%	25	32.5%	77
1885	6	7.2%	6	7.2%	26	31.3%	8	9.6%	8	9.6%	1	1.2%	28	33.7%	83
1890	8	7.2%	6	5.4%	27	24.3%	14	12.6%	10	9.0%	0	0.0%	46	41.4%	111
1895	8	6.9%	9	7.8%	23	19.8%	16	13.8%	10	8.6%	2	1.7%	48	41.4%	116
1900	6	6.5%	11	11.8%	23	24.7%	7	7.5%	5	5.4%	2	2.2%	39	41.9%	93
1905	9	10.8%	9	10.8%	23	27.7%	7	8.4%	3	3.6%	1	1.2%	34	41.0%	83
1910	8	10.0%	8	10.0%	13	16.3%	3	3.8%	4	5.0%	1	1.3%	43	53.8%	80
1914	10	14.3%	7	10.0%	10	14.3%	6	8.6%	4	5.7%	2	2.9%	31	44.3%	70
1920	9	13.8%	3	4.6%	16	24.6%	1	1.5%	3	4.6%	2	3.1%	31	47.7%	65

Table 2.2

Summary

The national federation of American Turners began formally supporting libraries in its official documents shortly after the founding of the organization. Libraries were one part of a concerted effort to educate the membership and families to become free-thinking, socially conscious citizens. The local Turner societies tried to follow the national directive of maintaining a library, however small. The value of society libraries was well-known to the German immigrant. The leadership of the American Turners wanted to ensure appropriate reading material for its membership. Their respect for the printed word was reflected in the production of their own national newspaper for the promotion of "radical" ideas and *Turnen*, and in the production of their own liberal schoolbooks.

As the Turners aged and became more conservative, less emphasis was placed on the role of libraries within the official Turner documents. The directive for a complete library of good literature and books on welfare and reform was changed to one recommending the purchase of texts specific to *Turnen*. This change coincided with the development of stronger German-language collections in public libraries with large German-speaking communities. A closer examination of this relationship is made in successive chapters. Statistical analysis of the data submitted to the American Turners' National Headquarters supports a relationship between the development of libraries and the number of Turner members in the early years, and later the age of the organization was a good predictor of library size. The older Turner organizations with sizeable memberships usually established libraries and maintained them through the period of this study. Many other factors, not related to the statistical information, also played a part, and these will be examined in later chapters.

The descriptive information contained in the following chapters focuses mainly on the *Turnbezirke* of this Midwestern region. Those societies with larger libraries or in major cities are covered more fully simply because their primary materials were more readily obtainable. Many primary materials are still in private hands and access to some sources was made primarily through serendipity. The later, excellent work of Pumroy and Rampelmann,[32] which surveys the availability of American Turner records, will ease the burden for others wishing to work with these materials. And, further research does indeed need to be done on the many communities identified to enhance our understanding of the statistical data available.

NOTES

[1]Charles E. McClelland, *State, Society, and University in Germany, 1700–1914* (New York: Cambridge University Press, 1980), 222.

[2]Ibid., 225.

[3]American Turners, Minutes of the National Conventions, 1854–1872, tr. Henry W. Kumpf, undated, Typescript, Special Collections & Archives, IUPUI University Library, Indianapolis, IN; American Turners, *Officialle Protokolle der Tagsatzungen des Nordamerikanischen Turnerbundes*, 1874–1900, Special Collections & Archives, IUPUI University Library, Indianapolis, IN.

[4]American Turners, Minutes of the National Convention, 1854, 28.

[5]Ibid., 1855, 57.

[6]Ibid.

[7]Ibid., 1854, 1; 1855, 41.

[8]Ibid., 1855, 71.

[9]Ibid., 70.

[10]Ibid., 1855/1856, 127. "Reports of the Executive Committees of the American Turners" were also included in and paginated with the translation of the "Minutes of the National Conventions."

[11]Ibid., 1857, 147.

[12]Ibid.

[13]Ibid., 1857/1858, 232. An interesting note in the 1858 Minutes of the National Convention in Indianapolis thanked the Indiana State Librarian for permission to use the Senate Hall for their convention site. Minutes, 1858, 229.

[14]Ibid., 1858, 242.

[15]Ibid., 1859, 262.

[16]Ibid., 265.

[17]Ibid., 1859, 345.

[18]Ibid., 1866, 399.

[19]Ibid., 405.

[20]Ibid., 406–07.

[21]Ibid., 1868, 445.

[22]Robert E. Cazden, *A Social History of the German Book Trade in America to the Civil War*, Studies in German Literature, Linguistics, and Culture, vol. 1 (Columbia, SC: Camden House, 1984), 290.

[23]American Turners, Minutes, 1868, 448.

[24]Ibid., 451.

[25]Ibid., 1871, 507.

[26]Ibid., 1870, 470.

[27]Ibid., 1874, 571.

[28]American Turners, *Platform, principielle Beschlüsse & Statuten des Nordamerikanischen Turnerbundes*, 1894, 5, in Wilmington Turngemeinde, *Platform, Constitution und Nebengesetze* (Wilmington, DE: Freie Presse, 1895), Wilmington Turners Lodge Collection, Research Library, Balch Institute for Ethnic Studies, Philadelphia, PA; American Turners, *Platform, prinzipielle Beschlüsse und Statuten des Nordamerikan. Turnerbundes*, 1896, 6, in Indianapolis Socialer Turnverein, *Constitution und Nebengesetze des Sozialen Turnvereins von Indianapolis, Ind. ...* (Indianapolis, IN: Druck der Tribüne Pub. Co., 1897), Special Collections & Archives, IUPUI University Library.

[29]American Turners, *Jahresberichte des Vororts des Nordamerikanischen Turnerbundes*, 1907/08, xxxvi, Special Collections & Archives, IUPUI University Library.

[30]American Turners, Statistik des Nordamerikanischen Turnerbundes, 1866–1873, Special Collections & Archives, IUPUI University Library,

Indianapolis, IN.

[31]Horst Ueberhorst, *Turner unterm Sternenbanner* (Munich: H. Moos, 1978), 43.

[32]Eric Pumroy and Katja Rampelmann, *Research Guide to the Turner Movement in the United States* (Westport, CT: Greenwood Press, 1996).

III

ADMINISTRATION OF TURNER LIBRARIES

The importance of libraries in an organization can be measured in part by the prominence of the library in official documents and indirectly by the administration of the library. How prominent is the library in the stated purpose of the organization? What is the administrative standing of the librarian or library committee? Are the duties of library administration specifically defined? What care is given to the library collection? How is the library funded? How accessible is the library? The answer to these questions fortifies the understanding of the role of these libraries within the Turner groups.

Statement of Purpose in Official Turner Documents

Of three printed constitution and bylaws obtained, two Turnvereins specifically mentioned libraries in their overall statements on purposes of the organizations. Both in the 1889 and 1895 "Freibrief der Wilmington Turngemeinde"[1] the stated purpose was the same. The 1895 version was given in English:

> The object of the said Corporation shall be the intellectual and physical improvement of the members by forming and keeping up a library, by establishing schools and by furnishing instruction in gymnastic exercises.[2]

In addition, in the Constitution of 1889 itself is a listing of "Rights and Duties of the Board Members." One duty defined was "i) Für Erweiterung der Bibliothek zu sorgen."[3] Although this listing was no longer given in 1895, Article 2 of that Constitution repeated the purpose of the *Verein*. The means to achieve the purpose were:

> Körperliche Turnübungen; Alle Arten Waffenübungen; Dramatische und gesellige Unterhaltung; Gesang, Bibliothek und Vorträge.[4]

For the Wilmington Turngemeinde the library officially remained a major objective within the organization as a means of intellectual development.

The New Ulm Turnverein of New Ulm, Minnesota, stated the purpose of its organization in the Bylaws of 1888:

> Der Zweck des Vereins ist Förderung körperlicher und geistiger
> Ausbildung und allgemeine Wirksamkeit im Sinne des entschiedenen
> Fortschrittes. Als Mittel hierzu werden betrachtet: . . . Beschaffung
> und Vermehrung einer guten Vereinsbibliothek und Pflege von Gesang
> und Musik . . .[5]

As in the case of Wilmington, the library was one of several means of achieving
the stated purpose of the Turnverein.

The Indianapolis Socialer Turnverein's stated purpose in the 1897
Constitution, however, contained nothing specific about libraries. Its general
purpose was similar to that of the others in building both the physical and the
mental capabilities of the individual to ensure a responsible, reform-minded
citizenry:

> . . . zu körperlich und geistig tüchtigen Menschen heranzubilden . . .
> dem Staate thatkräftige und gesinnungstüchtige Bürger heranzuziehen,
> welche stets bereit sind, heilsame Reformen mit Wort und That zu
> unterstützen.[6]

On the other hand, the "Statutes" of the Indianapolis Turn-Schwestern Verein
specifically stated under paragraph two, the purpose of the organization:

> Derselbe hat die Aufgabe, den Turnverein nach Kräften zu unterstützen,
> speziell aber die Mädchen-Turnschule zu hegen und zu überwachen und
> für die Vergrößerung und Erweiterung der Bibliothek und ihre
> allgemeine Benutzung im Verein zu wirken und bei allen geistigen und
> geselligen Bestrebungen des Vereins mitzuwirken.[7]

Increasing the use of the library as well as increasing the size of the library were
major goals stated for this ladies' auxiliary organization.

The same was true for the 1915 constitution of the St. Anthony Turnverein[8]
and the 1908 constitution of the Turnverein St. Paul,[9] both in Minnesota. Not
enough constitutions for this time period were located for the institutions studied
to generalize about the placement of libraries within the primary purpose
statement. However, it is clear that several, especially among the early ones, felt
the library was indeed instrumental to accomplishing the intellectual goals of their
organization, although the more recent the constitution, the less prominence the

library held in that statement. Whether the library was placed in the primary purpose statement or not, each Turner organization studied did mention elsewhere in the constitution and bylaws the role of a librarian or library committee within its administrative structure.

The Librarian or Library Committee in the Administration Hierarchy

The place of the librarian or the existence of a library committee as one of the standing committees within the administrative structure is a further clue to the importance the organization placed on this entity for its membership. With the limited primary documents available, no correlation could be found between the presence of the librarian as an officer of the executive board and the size of a library collection. However, the presence of a standing library committee was a more significant indicator in relation to size. For example, the larger library collections of the Cincinnati Turngemeinde and the New Ulm Turnverein were under the care of standing library committees, but the chairs of the committees were not officers. In the case of the Wilmington Turngemeinde and the Turnverein St. Paul, the librarian or chair of the library committee was a member of the executive board although neither of these organizations had a library of the proportions of the Cincinnati Turngemeinde. As might be expected, Turnvereins with no mention of a librarian or library committee in their official documents generally had very small collections, such as that of the West Seite Turnverein of St. Paul, Minnesota.

Duties of the Librarian or Library Committee

The specific duties of the librarian or library committee were frequently recorded in the bylaws of the Turner organizations, but with varying amounts of detail. The librarians or committees were generally members elected to these posts. The Wilmington 1889 bylaws clearly stated that the office of librarian was an honorary one, not receiving pay.[10] This was usually the case for all officials in the Turnvereins. Library committees varied from three (New Ulm) to five members (Cincinnati). It also was not unusual to have a second librarian, or "helping" librarian, assigned, as in the case of the Indianapolis Socialer Turnverein. The St. Louis Turnverein had two librarians named in the introduction to its 1880 catalog, and the half-year reports of the Milwaukee Turn-Zöglingsverein were signed by both librarians.

Normally official reports to the executive boards on the status of the library were mandated for every six months. Occasionally more frequent reports were demanded. When the Wilmington Turngemeinde added a library standing committee to the 1895 bylaws instead of just a librarian, the chair of that committee (who was also the librarian) was instructed to provide monthly reports to the executive committee as well as a yearly report to the Speaker, or chief executive.[11] Final reports at the end of one's term were also expected. These reports consisted of the number of books and "*Schriften*" owned, the number of books loaned, and the general status of the collection. Unfortunately, very few of these reports survived. Usually the minutes of the Turners recorded only that the reports were received and approved.

Although official reports were normally on a six-month cycle, bills for the libraries were often recorded in the minutes of the organization since all accounts had to be approved by the executive boards, or their designee, for payment. The *Vorstand* kept tight reins on financial matters. Also, in the case of the Cincinnati Turngemeinde, further oversight into the affairs of the library by the *Vorstand* were evident in the minutes.[12] A few of these examples are: in the 14 January 1860 minutes the Library Committee members were instructed to be present when the library was open; on 3 December 1861, the *Vorstand* demanded that the Library Committee put the Library in order immediately; on 18 May 1862, the Library Committee was requested to recommend which journals could be eliminated "*ohne Nachteil*"; on 6 December 1865, the Library Committee was asked to investigate where the two copies of the *Criminalzeitung* disappeared to each year; and on 27 August 1866, the Library Committee was asked to consider purchases from a list of books for sale from Edward Buhler of Chicago. Such statements indicate that there was more than a passing interest in the affairs of the library. The greater frequency of mention of library affairs in minutes seems to correspond with those organizations having larger libraries, and also with the earlier years of the group.

Inventories, marking of volumes, lists of books loaned, and returned, collection of fine monies, ordering and receiving books, and production of catalogs were among the duties mentioned in various bylaws. Many of these items will be discussed more fully later.

Organization and Maintenance of the Library Collection

Housing. Larger Turner libraries consisted of both a library room and a reading room. The reading room would contain current newspapers and journal issues. Illustration 3.1 is a copy of an older photograph of such a 1898 reading room in Das Deutsche Haus, Indianapolis.[13] This room was shared by all the members of the building under the umbrella name of Der Deutsche Klub. The Indianapolis Socialer Turnverein was the largest organization occupying Das Deutsche Haus and actually sponsored the building through the Socialer Turnverein Stock Association. Illustration 3.2 is a 1898 floor plan showing the location of the

Der Deutsche Club—Lesezimmer/Reading Room

Reading Room of Das Deutsche Haus,
Indianapolis, 1898

Illustration 3.1

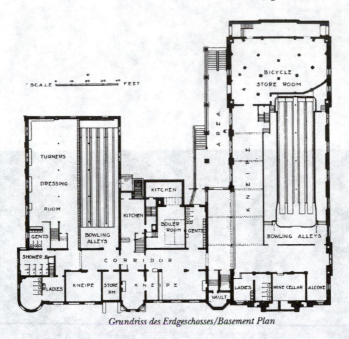

Grundriss des Erdgeschosses/Basement Plan

Floor Plan of Das Deutsche Haus, Indianapolis

Grundriss des zweiten Stockwerks/Second Floor Plan

Illustration 3.2

library for the Indianapolis Socialer Turnverein.[14] This was later to become the home of the Normal College of the American Turners and house the College library.

The Building Committee of the Cincinnati Turngemeinde resolved in October 1858 to provide "ein geraumiges Bibliotheks- und Lesezimmer" in the new building.[15] Later minutes in 1860 and again in 1864 reported moves of the library room. On 24 January 1866 a motion was passed to have a new bookcase built for the library at a cost from $60 to $65, a substantial sum for this time period.

The Aurora Turnverein of Chicago rented and furnished two rooms to be used as library and reading rooms in 1884 according to Keil and Jentz, important research scholars on German-Americans in Chicago.[16]

A separate room for a library was also provided by the New Ulm Turnverein, but the minutes reported several conflicts in use. On 9 February 1873 a motion was passed by the Library Committee to ask the cloak-room attendant to clean up the library room on those occasions when it was used as a cloak-room.[17] Later that year the Verein decided that a room in the new building would be designated for the library.[18] There must have been further conflicts in use since in 1889 it was resolved that the library space should be used only for library-related purposes.[19] A little more than a year later the *Verein* agreed to allow Sunday School classes to be held in the library room.[20] These classes apparently were considered consistent with the purpose of the library.

Other Turnvereins supplied little more than a book case or two to house their collections. Such was the case in Madison, Wisconsin, and in St. Paul, Minnesota, for the West Seite Turnverein, where the library of 87 books was housed in one book case in the meeting room.[21]

Classification and catalogs. A number of different classification or arrangement schemes were used for the Turner library collections. The simplest arrangement of a collection was not a classified one, but a straight numbering of volumes as received. This is a method still employed by some major European libraries with closed stacks such as the Herzog August Bibliothek in Wolfenbüttel, Germany. Others combined a letter for a major grouping, and then employed numbers within that grouping. At times the numbers assigned within that class attempted to establish an alphabetical order within a class. It was not unusual to find evidence that books were renumbered to correspond to a new system. Most Turner libraries had some catalog or listing of books available to members. The catalogs were either alphabetically arranged by author or classified by broad subject areas.

The arrangement and order of the collection was a recurring topic for discussion in the Library Committee of the New Ulm Turnverein. As early as 11 February 1869 a proposal was passed to number the books and complete a catalog. The Secretary of the Library Committee was charged with finding the appropriate marking system for this purpose.[22] Again in 1871 the Library Committee resolved to number the library books and "write" a catalog.[23] It is not clear if the first resolution was not carried out or if it was simply time for new acquisitions to be marked and a new catalog completed. Once again in 1872 the Library Committee passed a motion "to complete the numbering of works as started in the catalog arranged by C. Baer."[24] In the 1888 Constitution and Bylaws of the New Ulm Turnverein, the Library Committee was clearly charged with the responsibility of providing an "index to books and writings."[25] Neither the catalog nor enough of the books have survived to provide a sense of the collection arrangement.

The remnants of the Milwaukee Turnverein and Indianapolis Socialer Turnverein were usually marked simply with accession numbers on the spine. Multiple volumes of a set or series were marked with successive numbers, but for the Milwaukee Turnverein there were occasionally lower-case letters following the numbers, perhaps to fit successive volumes in with the same title when not enough numbers were left for additions between titles. The Milwaukee Turnverein collection was so disordered by the time of this research, that no clear pattern of arrangement could be ascertained.

Catalogs of Turner library collections did survive in at least three instances, Wilmington, Cincinnati, and St. Louis, providing more concrete evidence of arrangement. The St. Louis Turnverein 1895 catalog provided an alphabetical listing of works by author, or by title in the case of periodical publications.[26] At times the titles were entered by a *Schlagwort* in the title rather than the first non-article word, e.g. "Krieg. Der deutsch-französische."[27] Such *Schlagwörter* entries are common for German bibliographies. The original printed numbers in the catalog showed an attempt to keep volumes of an author together in one numbering sequence. However, this was not always achieved. For example, in the case of Berthold Auerbach, the first three titles were clustered under the numbers, 925–31. The following titles were originally numbered 1339–55. These may have been the clusters in which they were purchased, but obviously the items were not numbered consecutively (see Illustration 3.3). These same entries also provide a good example of how the library collections were renumbered. The first multi-volume title was renumbered 1356–62 in what appeared to be an attempt to gather all the works of this author in one sequence. However, other assigned numbers which were crossed out and resupplied do not fit into the same sequence. It would be difficult to analyze the arrangement

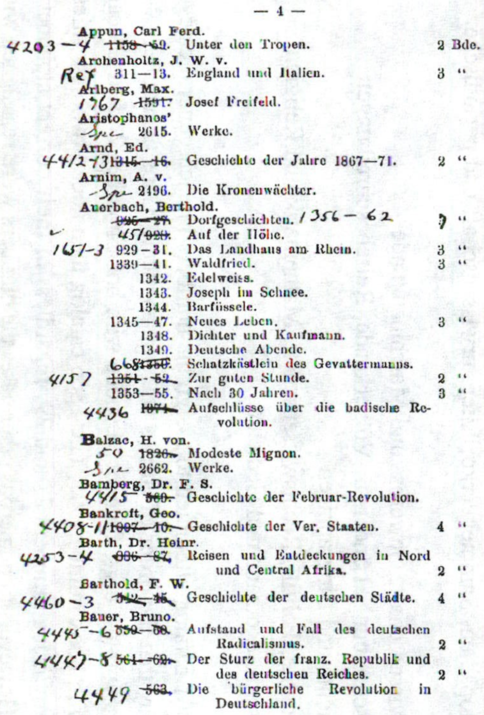

— 4 —

Appun, Carl Ferd.
4203-4 1138-40. Unter den Tropen. 2 Bde.

Arnholz, J. W. v.
Ref. 311-13. England und Italien. 3 "

Athens, Max.
1767-1817 Josef Freifeld.

Antophanes'
Spec. 2615. Werke.

Arndt, Ed.
4441-3 1844-46 Geschichte der Jahre 1867-71. 2 "

Arnim, A. v.
Spec. 2196. Die Kronenwächter.

Auerbach, Berthold.
455-27 457992 Dorfgeschichten. 1356-62 7 "
167-3 929-31. Auf der Höhe. 3 "
1339-41. Das Landhaus am Rhein. 3 "
1342. Waldfried.
1343. Edelweiss.
1344. Joseph im Schnee.
Barfüssele.
1345-47. Neues Leben. 3 "
1348. Dichter und Kaufmann.
1349. Deutsche Abende.
4057 2631-32 Schatzkästlein des Gevattermanns. 2 "
4261-62 Zur guten Stunde. 2 "
1353-55. Nach 30 Jahren. 3 "
4436 441 Aufschlüsse über die badische Revolution.

Balzac, H. von Modeste Mignon.
Spec. 2885. Werke.

Bamberg, Dr. F. S.
Spec. 2662.
4415 869 Geschichte der Februar-Revolution. 4 "

Bancroft, Geo.
4408-1/1697-10. Geschichte der Ver. Staaten.

Barth, Dr. Heinr.
4203-4 655-57. Reisen und Entdeckungen in Nord und Central Afrika. 2 "

Berthold, F. W.
4460-3 441-46. Geschichte der deutschen Städte. 4 "

Bauer, Bruno.
4448-6 659-69. Aufstand und Fall des deutschen Radicalismus. 2 "
4445-8 661-69. Der Sturz der franz. Republik und des deutschen Reiches. 2 "
4449 663. Die bürgerliche Revolution in Deutschland.

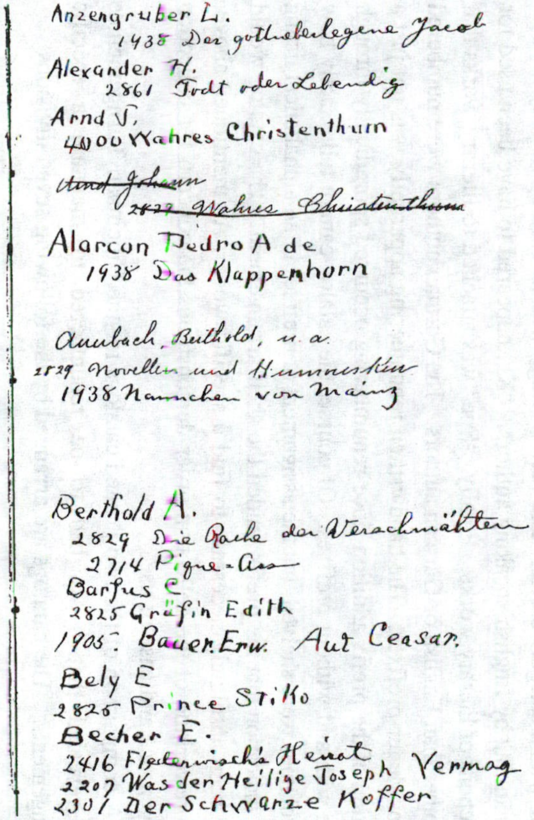

Anzengruber L.
1438 Der gottabgelegene Jacob

Alexander H.
2861 Todt oder Lebendig

Arnd J.
4800 Wahres Christenthum

Adolf Johnson
1862 Wahres Christenthum

Alarcon Pedro A de
1438 Das Klappenhorn

Auerbach Berthold, u. a.
1439 Novellen und Humoresken
1938 Nannchen von Mainz

Berthold A.
1829 Die Rache der Verachteten
2714 Pique-Cas
Barfüs
2825 Gräfin Edith
1905 Bauer, Ern. Aut Ceasar.

Bely E
2826 Prince St.Ko

Becher E.
2416 Fledermaus Heint
2207 Was der Heilige Joseph Vermag
2307 Der schwarze Koffer

Pages From the St. Louis Turnverein
Library Catalog, 1895

Illustration 3.3

thoroughly without completely re-sorting all the catalog entries by number.

There also may have been an attempt to sort the titles by a general classification since the handwritten renumbering included letter prefixes, e.g., Spe, Eng, Kl, W, X, Ref. "Ref" was obviously for reference titles. "X" was used for journal titles. "W" seemed to have been used for non-literary works not falling within categories "Ref" and "X." "Eng" was entered by literary titles in German, but by English-speaking authors. "Kl" appeared to have been used for collections of literary works. Finally, "Spe" was attached to literary works that had other than English or German authors. The German authors were numbered without letter prefixes. The handwritten renumbering apparently was not just a function of the prefix addition since renumbering occurred sporadically through those with and without prefixes. Of course, the catalog cannot tell exactly how the volumes were shelved, but the assignment of prefixes in an alphabetical listing is an indication that the prefix guided the shelf arrangement. The catalog would have been absolutely necessary to find a specific work. As mentioned above, such reworking of the collection order demonstrates the concern for collection maintenance and ease of use.

A comparison of the two printed catalogs for the Cincinnati Turngemeinde also revealed that books had to be renumbered to maintain a specific arrangement.[28] The catalogs are arranged by the following seven divisions:

   I. Turnen und Gymnastik
  II. Encyclopädien, Sammelwerke, Literaturwissenschaft und periodische Schriften
 III. Naturwissenschaft, Gewerbs- und Maschinenkunde
  IV. Erdbeschreibung, Länder- u. Völkerkunde, Reisebeschreibungen
   V. Geschichte und Biographieen
  VI. Philosophie, Politik, Rechtswissenschaft, Mathematik und Religion
 VII. Belletristik, Romane und Gedichte

The 1861 catalog attempted to assign the numbers in each general category in such a way that the order of entries was alphabetical. Gaps of numbers were left to add new titles, e.g., Category I ended with book number 26 and Category II started with book number 50. The 1866 catalog then added two new titles to Category I by using numbers 27 and 29, regardless of their correct alphabetical sequence. However, in numerous other cases the numbers were reassigned within a category to provide an alphabetical order. At times this must have been considered too tedious a task so a title would be inserted in the right part of the alphabet, although not strictly alphabetically. Thus, the authors Geibel and

Gottlieb (numbers 338–41) were sandwiched between *Grundriß der Naturlehre* (no author, number 337) and the author Guyot (number 342). If the books were shelved in numerical order, a classified arrangement would have resulted with the authors roughly alphabetical within that classification. The handwritten entries added to the 1866 catalog seem to indicate that this arrangement had been abandoned as they were entered sequentially without regard to subject matter or to alphabetical arrangement. The categories used by the Cincinnati Turngemeinde reflect a greater concern about subject divisions than the later revisions of the St. Louis Turnverein, which used the category "W" for what Cincinnati designated as classes III, IV, V, and VI.

The Wilmington Turngemeinde catalog also presented a classified arrangement and a more complex numbering system. The classifications given were:

C   Classicker [sic], Ballade und Gedichte
B   Geschichte, Geographie, Reisebeschreibung und wissenschaftliche
      Literatur
D   Zeitschriften
E   Romane und Novellen
H   Bücher in englischer Sprache
V   Vermischte Literatur

These categories align more closely with the St. Louis scheme than that of the Cincinnati Turngemeinde. Category "V" was truly an eclectic one, and many later entries appear to have been tacked on to this category rather than added to their original designations.

The volumes themselves had running numbers as well as assigned numbers within their categories. Both appeared on the spines of the volumes. The numbering was not an attempt to keep the titles in alphabetical order since Schiller's works were the first under class "C," followed by Goethe's works. An attempt was made to keep works of an author together. If a later volume was added to a title, but the next number was already used, "1/2" might be used following the last number of an author to keep that author's works in order. The 1895 bylaws of the Wilmington Turngemeinde specifically instructed the Library Committee to maintain a list of the books and writings of the library and that no book was to be lent out until it was stamped with the ownership and entered in a list.[29]

Obviously the Turner library caretakers were concerned about the broad classifications of their collections, but specifically numbering each volume in an accession-type style caused them problems as they grew in size. Some approached this problem by renumbering the whole collection. It was not unknown among public libraries at this time to also change approaches to classification. For example, Charles Evans, director of the Indianapolis Public Library, set about having the collection reclassed in 1889 to accommodate a larger size collection, using a classification scheme of Poole.[30] This reclassification involved renumbering the entire collection.

Binding and repair. The physical maintenance of its collection is another indicator of a library's importance to an organization. Many of the Turnvereins recorded in their minutes the payment of bills to book binders. Such binding was for both books and journals. Many German-language books were issued in *Lieferungen* during the nineteenth century and left to be bound by the subscriber.[31] The minutes from the New Ulm Turnverein Library Committee frequently mentioned the recommendations of purchases that should be made and then bound. In some cases they were the entire work, in other cases, reference was to the completion of signatures:

> 15 September 1869
> *beschlossen* . . . Ferner, nachzufragen ob fehlende Lieferungen von Spencer's Geschichte der Vereinigten Staaten (Prachtausgabe) zu bekommen seien.
>
> 21 September 1871
> *beschlossen* Die Werke von Aurbach anzuschafen [sic] und einbinden [sic] zu lassen.
> *beschlossen* Die Lieferung des Illustrirtes Thierleben anzuschaffen und einbinden zu lassen.
> *beschlossen* Das Deutsch Englische Conversation Lexikon anzuschaffen und einzubinden.[32]

Similar comments were found in the Cincinnati Turngemeinde minutes. For example, the Library Committee was asked in May 1860 to collect all valuable periodicals in the reading room and have them bound, and in January 1866 books that were received on *Turnen* from the *Vorort* for the *Bezirksvorstand* were delivered to the Library Committee for binding.[33] Many such examples could be cited from the minutes of the various Turner organizations.

Loan books. The general practice for recording loans seems to have required a ledger volume containing one page per person on which was entered each item loaned, the loan date, and return date. Illustration 3.4 shows such a page from the Wilmington Turngemeinde "Library Borrowers' Record Book."[34] The same methodology was described by the Library Committee of the New Ulm Turnverein:

> Beschlossen jedem Mitglied des Vereins eine Seite in den Büchern anzuweisen, auf welcher die Entgegennahme u. Ablieferung v. Bücher, einfach durch Einschreibung des Datums debitirt und creditirt werden solle.[35]

Funding

Funding for Turner libraries varied greatly. Obviously, larger Turner libraries must have been better financed, but frequently the method of such financing was not directly mentioned in the minutes or bylaws. Two Turner organizations that provided specific references to funding in their bylaws were the Wilmington Turngemeinde and the Indianapolis Socialer Turnverein. The Wilmington Turngemeinde stated in its 1895 bylaws that the Library Committee could spend money for purchases up to an amount stipulated each year by the society. The amount was left blank and would have been supplied for each given year.[36] The Indianapolis Socialer Turnverein stated the following in its 1897 constitution:

> Fünf   Prozent   der   jährlichen   Mitgliederbeiträge   sind   zu Neuanschaffungen und Instandhaltung der Bibliothek zu verwenden.[37]

While a stipulated yearly amount for the library sounds reassuring, the resultant funds available were meager. The dues recorded in the 1897 bylaws were six dollars per member. The 1900 national statistics reported 220 members. At five percent there would be sixty-six dollars available for the library. In contrast the Cincinnati Turngemeinde expended ninety-five dollars for purchases in 1875.[38] From 1900 to 1905 the increase in library holdings for the Indianapolis Socialer Turnverein was only nine volumes even though the membership increased from 220 to 250. Unless the monies designated for the library were spent for book cases, binding or other related items, the library volumes added did not reflect the amount designated by the 1897 formula.

No printed constitution was discovered for the Cincinnati Turngemeinde, but the minutes of 23 April 1859 reveal that some monies for the library were received from new members' initiation dues, fines, and sales of catalogs. Benefit

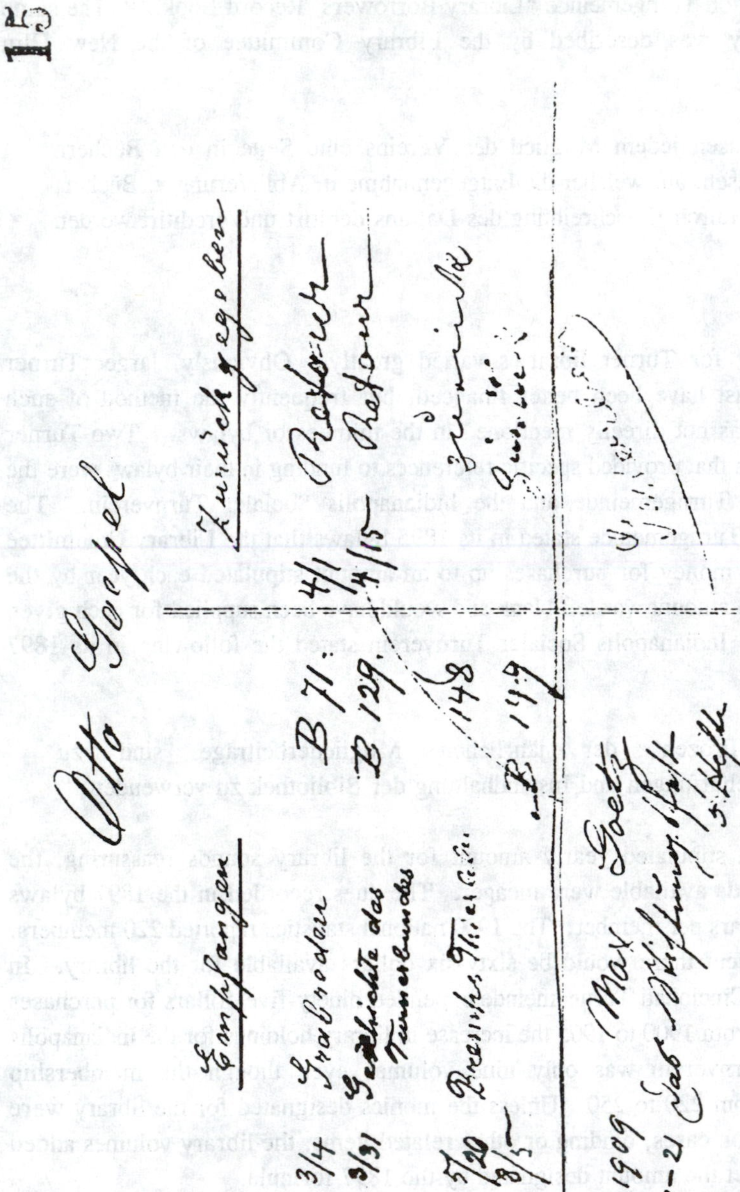

Illustration 3.4

activities were also held to raise money for the library. The same was true for the New Ulm Turnverein. On 18 February 1875 the New Ulm Library Committee passed a motion to ask the Verein to give a theater production for the benefit of the library. Theater productions of the Turnverein were well attended in New Ulm. Apparently the New Ulm Library Committee also experienced difficulties at times in obtaining the funds designated for it. On 9 February 1873 the Library Committee passed a resolution requesting the Turnverein to deliver the money due to the Library according to the Constitution for the completion of the Library and the purchase of magazines for the reading room. Indeed, according to the 6 March 1875 minutes of the main body of the Turnverein, the binding of damaged books was asked to be postponed until the financial situation of the Verein improved. And on 10 October 1875, the Library Committee recorded that the Verein would not support the purchase of books from M. Henschel because of low cash on hand.

Some other Turner libraries of this period reported more substantial regular support of their collections. The Chicago Turngemeinde Library reported a yearly expenditure of $250 and a yearly addition of 125 volumes in 1875.[39] In the same year the St. Louis Turnverein reported $300 yearly were expended on library purchases for 200 volumes a year.[40]

Obviously the methods and amount of funding for libraries varied considerably from one Turner organization to another.

Hours of Operation

The hours which the Turner libraries were open reflected the fact that the Turner organizations were composed primarily of working people whose main access would need to be evenings and weekends. Since most people also worked on Saturday, Sunday would have been the main weekend day for use. For these same reasons, many Turner activities took place on Sunday when their membership could attend. The librarian or members of the library committee were required to be in attendance to serve the members. The hours of library operation were occasionally spelled out in the bylaws themselves, but frequently they were simply part of the general rules for the library. The Wilmington Turngemeinde specified in its 1897 Constitution that the chair of the library committee was responsible for opening the library for exchange of books at least once a week for an hour.[41] The Indianapolis Socialer Turnverein stipulated that the library was to be open to members at any time.[42]

In 1872 the New Ulm Turnverein library expanded its hours from Thursday evenings from 8 to 10 p.m. and Sunday mornings from 9 a.m. to 12 noon in 1871 to every evening of the week as well as Sunday mornings.[43] A member of the

Library Committee was to be there to conduct business when the library was open.

The Milwaukee Turnverein library's bookplate presented the rules of the library, including the fact that the library was to be open at least once a week for the use and loan of books.

The Cincinnati Turngemeinde library was very generous in its accessibility. As early as 1860 the library and reading room were available every evening except Saturday and Sunday, although they were open Sunday afternoons. A member of the Library Committee was to be present "um die verlangten Schriften verabfolgen zu lassen."[44] The Library Committee was allowed to add members to meet these requirements.

The reading rooms, containing current newspapers and journals, were more accessible since these materials were used within the room and did not require a member to sign out materials.

By comparison, a number of public libraries started opening on Sundays in the 1870s (Cincinnati, 1871; Indianapolis, 1873; St. Louis, 1872), although their hours during the week were much more generous than those of the Turner libraries. Because of the general anti-clerical stance of the early Turners, Sunday hours were not controversial. In fact, Sundays would have been considered an appropriate time for self-education and improvement to be judiciously blended with celebrations and various forms of entertainment.

Loan Restrictions and Fines

The loan period most frequently encountered in this study was for fourteen days with extensions of varying amounts allowed, often only with permission of the librarian. The Cincinnati Turngemeinde allowed the usual fourteen days but "ein Buch streng wissenschaftlichen Inhalts [darf] vier Wochen behalten werden."[45] The most generous loan period was for four weeks, with extensions from four to eight weeks more. Several Turnvereins (Indianapolis, Aurora) allowed only one book to be checked out at a time. New Ulm Turnverein permitted two books at a time to be signed out. Some other Turner libraries did not stipulate the number of books that could be loaned per member. The loan book from Wilmington listed from three to four volumes at a time per single loan date for a member.

In every case the member was responsible for the replacement or cost of any damaged or lost book. Fines from five to ten cents a week were imposed for overdue books. Library privileges could usually be withheld from members who did not pay their fines.

Bookplates were normally inserted in each volume containing the rules for use of the library and the number of the book.

Summary

The formal recognition given the Turner libraries in their official documents attested to their importance in the organization. The best indicator that the library had some prominence within the Turner organizations was the specification of a librarian or library committee in the constitution or bylaws. Concern for arrangement and maintenance of the collection was another indicator of the importance of this investment for the Turner organizations. Such concern might be expressed by rules specifically stated in the bylaws or indirectly through instructions given to the library committees in the minutes of the Turnverein. Rules for library operation were very similar to those of other libraries of that time period. While the hours open were not as generous as some society and public libraries at that time, the hours did reflect volunteer operations serving the hours their clientele had available. Also, from their inception the Turner libraries were generally open on Sundays since the early Turner organizations were anti-clerical in nature and considered Sundays an opportunity for education as well as entertainment.

NOTES

[1]Wilmington Turngemeinde, *Constitution und Nebengesetze* (Wilmington, DE: Freie Presse, 1889); Wilmington Turngemeinde, *Platform, Constitution und Nebengesetze* (Wilmington, DE: Freie Presse, 1895), Wilmington Turners Lodge Collection, Research Library, Balch Institute for Ethnic Studies, Philadelphia, PA.

[2]Wilmington Turngemeinde, *Platform* (1895), 33.

[3]Wilmington Turngemeinde, *Constitution* (1889), 12.

[4]Wilmington Turngemeinde, *Platform* (1895), 35.

[5]New Ulm Turverein, *Platform und principielle Beschluesse des Nordamerikanischen Turnerbundes, sowie Verfassung, Nebengesetze und stehende Beschluesse des New-Ulmer Turnvereins*, 18 August 1888 (New Ulm, MN: Druck der "New Ulm Review," 1888), 11, pasted in New Ulm Turnverein, Protokoll Buch, 21 Juli 1888, New Ulm Turnverein, New Ulm, MN.

[6]Indianapolis Socialer Turnverein, *Constitution und Nebengesetze des Sozialen Turnvereins* ... (Indianapolis, IN: Druck der Tribüne Pub. Co., 1897), 32–33, Special Collections and Archives, IUPUI University Library, Indianapolis, IN.

[7]Indianapolis Turn-Schwestern Verein, *Statuten* (N.p., n.d.), 1, Inserted inside front cover of Account Book, Indianapolis Turn-Schwestern Verein, 1876–1883, Special Collections & Archives, IUPUI University Library.

[8]St. Anthony Turnverein, *Constitution und Nebengesetze des St. Anthony Turnvereins ... 1. Januar 1915* (Minneapolis, MN: Printed by Chronicle Pub. Co., 1915), St. Anthony Turnverein Records, Minnesota Historical Society, Minneapolis, MN.

[9]Turnverein St. Paul, *Verfassung und Nebengesetze des Turnverein "St. Paul."* (St. Paul, MN: Volkszeitung, 1908?), Minnesota Historical Society.

[10]Wilmington Turngemeinde, *Constitution* (1889), 15. The only officer to receive reimbursement for *"Zeitverlust"* (time spent) was the *"zweite Schriftwart"* (second Secretary).

[11]Wilmington Turngemeinde, *Platform* (1895), 46.

[12]Cincinnati Turngemeinde, Minutes, 1856-1936, Cincinnati Historical Society, Cincinnati, OH.

[13]Theodor Stempfel, *Fünfzig Jahre unermüdlichen Deutschen Strebens in Indianapolis*, German/English ed., eds. Giles R. Hoyt et al. (Indianapolis, IN: German-American Center and Indiana German Heritage Society, 1991), 77.

[14]Ibid., 104.

[15]Cincinnati Turngemeinde, Minutes, 23 October 1858.

[16]Harmut Keil and John B. Jentz, eds., *German Workers in Chicago: A Documentary History of Working Class Culture from 1850 to World War I* (Urbana, IL: University of Illinois Press, 1988), 166.

[17]New Ulm Turnverein, Library Committee, "Protokoll Buch des Bibliothek Comittees," 9 February 1873, Brown County Historical Museum, New Ulm, MN.

[18]Ibid., 9 November 1873.

[19]New Ulm Turnverein, Protokolle, 4 May 1889, New Ulm Turner Hall, New Ulm, MN.

[20]Ibid., 18 October 1890.

[21]West Seite Turnverein, Inventories, 1902, Minnesota Historical Society, Minneapolis, MN.

[22]New Ulm Turnverein, Library Committee, 11 February 1869.

[23]Ibid., 27 July 1871.

[24]Ibid., 25 July 1872.

[25]New Ulm Turnverein, *Platform*, 20.

[26]St. Louis Turnverein, *Katalog der Bibliothek des St. Louis Turnvereins* (St. Louis, MO: Aug. Wiebusch Printing Co., 1895), Special Collections,

Washington University Libraries, St. Louis, MO.

[27]Ibid., 25.

[28]Cincinnati Turngemeinde, *Katalog der Bibliothek der Turngemeinde in Cincinnati, April 1861* (Cincinnati, OH: Gedruckt bei Friedrich Lang, 1861), Cincinnati Historical Society, Cincinnati, OH; Cincinnati Turngemeinde, *Katalog der Bibliothek der Turn-Gemeinde in Cincinnati, O.* (Cincinnati, OH: Gedruckt bei Ad. Frey, 1866), Library of Congress, Washington, DC.

[29]Wilmington Turngemeinde, *Platform* (1895), 46.

[30]Thomas V. Hull, "The Origin and Development of the Indianapolis Public Library, 1873–1899" (M.A. thesis, University of Kentucky, 1956), 41.

[31]Robert E. Cazden, *A Social History of the German Book Trade in America to the Civil War*, Studies in German Literature, Linguistics, and Culture, vol. 1 (Columbia, SC: Camden House, 1984), 377.

[32]New Ulm Turngemeinde, Library Committee, 15 September 1869; 21 September 1871.

[33]Cincinnati Turngemeinde, Minutes, 23 May 1860; 24 January 1866.

[34]Wilmington Turngemeinde, Library Borrowers Record Book, 1906–1924, Wilmington Turners Lodge Collection, Research Library of the Balch Institute for Ethnic Studies, Philadelphia, PA.

[35]New Ulm Turnverein, Library Committee, 11 February 1869.

[36]Wilmington Turngemeinde, *Platform* (1895), 46.

[37]Indianapolis Socialer Turnverein, *Constitution*, 46.

[38]U.S. Bureau of Education, *Public Libraries in the United States of America: Their History, Condition, and Management: Special Report* (Washington, D.C.: GPO, 1876; reprint, Totowa, NJ: Rowman & Littlefield, 1971), 1107.

[39]*Public Libraries*, 1027.

[40]Ibid., 1074.

[41]Wilmington Turngemeinde, *Platform* (1895), 46.

[42]Indianapolis Socialer Turnverein, *Constitution*, 45.

[43]New Ulm Turnverein, Library Committee, 27 July 1871; 25 July 1872.

[44]Cincinnati Turngemeinde, Minutes, 14 January 1860.

[45]Cincinnati Turngemeinde, *Katalog* (1866), 3.

IV

CONTENT

Examining the contents of American Turner libraries as total collections was not always possible. Many collections no longer exist or only partially survived. Catalogs of these libraries were equally elusive although minutes of the various organizations indicated that some type of catalog had usually existed. The researcher was fortunate in discovering the remnants of several collections: The Louisville Turngemeinde (Kentucky),[1] the Lawrence Turnverein (Kansas), The Aurora Turnverein (Chicago, Illinois),[2] the Wilmington Turngemeinde (Delaware), and the Milwaukee Turnverein (Wisconsin).[3] In addition, the catalogs of several organizations were located: Cincinnati Turngemeinde (Ohio), 1861 and 1866 with handwritten additions until at least 1871;[4] the St. Louis Turnverein, 1895, with handwritten additions;[5] and the handwritten Wilmington Turngemeinde catalog, undated.[6]

The Lawrence Turnverein and Wilmington Turngemeinde collections are out of the primary scope of this study, but both provide supporting evidence of similarity in collections. The Lawrence Turnverein library was described with a full list of remnant holdings in a 1993 Masters thesis.[7] It provided the holdings of a smaller city Turnverein, that of one with 10,899 residents in 1885, which included 1,009 foreign-born.[8] The Wilmington Turngemeinde collection was included because it was the only one for which a borrowers' record book was located. Loan analysis and its relation to content for the Wilmington Turngemeinde is extensively discussed in the later chapter on usage.

Content will be examined for each Turner organization listed above. Comparison was done on a title basis instead of volumes since it was not always certain how many volumes of any given title were existent especially when dealing with remnants of collections. A title is defined for the purposes of this study as one bibliographic entry. The researcher used the entries as given in the various catalogs, or in the case of remnants of library collections, the entries as found in a national bibliographic utility, OCLC. This means that at times an author's works are considered as one entry even if comprising many individual titles. The form of entry used in catalogs took precedence since that was the way in which the organization considered the titles. Multiple copies of a single title were considered one title whereas different editions of the same title were considered separately. Broad categories will be defined for each, and then specific overlap of non-literature titles will be examined. It is the non-literature categories which would have defined the more educational and political characteristics of the collections. The holdings of the Turner libraries will also be compared with the contemporary German-language collections of two public libraries, the St. Louis Public Library and the Indianapolis Public Library. The German-language collections were the basis of comparison with the public libraries since the Turner libraries were primarily in German. These comparisons will provide information on similarities or differences of Turner libraries, while indicating to what extent the public library collections provided the same offerings. This content analysis will aid in the understanding of the purpose of these collections and the reasons for their demise.

Categories for Comparison

The following categories for comparison were chosen because they are categories which were frequently found in the library catalogs themselves:

Arts	Philosophy
Encyclopedias	Politics
General	Reference
History	School Books
Law	Science/Industry/Business
Literature:	Sports
World Literature	Travel & Geography
American Literature	Turner
English Literature	
French Literature	
German Literature	

The "Arts" include all the fine arts, primarily music, dance, and art. Theater works were usually the plays themselves and were included under literature. "Encyclopedias" and "Reference" contain only titles more general in nature. More specific works were considered under the subject covered. Thus, the multi-volume title, *Das Neue Buch der Erfindungen, Gewerbe und Industrien*, was considered under "Science," not "Encyclopedias" or "Reference." "General" was used to place works which did not easily fit into specific categories such as *Sammlung gemeinverständlicher wissenschaftlicher Vorträge*, which contained essays of science, history, and art. Journals which were general in nature were also put in this category. "History" contains biographical works as well as history.

"Literature" was divided by the researcher into more specific areas since this was the largest category for all collections, and such divisions provided greater insight into the types of literature collected and the number of translations into German. "German Literature" was defined by the researcher as any author whose native language was German. This would have included German-American authors. Tolzmann gives the arguments for a definition of German-American authorship in the preface to his work, *German-American Literature*.[9] A closer analysis of German-American authors as compared to German-European authors is a topic for further study although some comments on this relationship are offered by the researcher during the comparison. "American Literature" is defined as English-language American authors such as James Fenimore Cooper and Nathaniel Hawthorne. "World Literature" comprises all other languages and nationalities not specifically mentioned, including Latin. Notes on whether the literary works were in the original language or translation are given for each collection. Obviously, in the case of the two public libraries all the titles would be in German translation since these catalogs only represented the German-language works.

"Philosophy" comprised works that pertain also to analysis of religious topics. The Turners, at least in their early period, were considered rationalists and often collected works dealing with a rationalist or deist examination of religious themes as opposed to religious doctrinal tracts. For the public library collections "Philosophy" does include works on religion although they are often less controversial.

"School Books" are included separately since they were found in the remnants of a few collections. However, Turners frequently had separate libraries for younger Turners, such as in Milwaukee, Aurora, and Cincinnati, and the catalogs found do not reflect those collections.

"Science" as a category reflects both pure and applied science, agriculture, business, and industry. This is a combined category for several Turner libraries such as Cincinnati.

"Sports" includes such topics as games and fishing. Books related more specifically to Turner activities such as gymnastics and Turner histories are entered under "Turner."

"Travel and Geography" contains the many popular books written on travel as well as descriptions of cultures.

Remnants of Turner Library Collections

Lawrence Turnverein, Lawrence, Kansas. The remaining volumes of the Lawrence Turnverein collection are listed by Rampelmann.[10] These volumes represent 32.8%, or 82 out of the 250 volumes, reported for 1919/20 to the national Turner headquarters. Charts 4.1 and 4.2 show graphically the relative proportions by subject categories. Of the 37 titles present, 35 are in German and two in English. The two English titles are a 1926 volume of *The Gymnast*, the yearbook of the Normal College of the American Turnerbund, and a volume of *Papers Relating to Foreign Affairs Accompanying the Annual Message of the President to the First Session, Thirty-Ninth Congress*, Part III (1866). The latter was the only federal government document listed. Most of the Turner collections examined contained some United States government documents, showing their interest in staying abreast of government activities. For this reason, most of the federal documents found were aligned with the category "Politics." The most currently dated title held was that of *The Gymnast*. Otherwise, no titles are dated later than 1894. The longest run of a journal, *Die Deutsche Roman-Zeitung*, was held from 1869 to 1876. Even though the volumes found do not represent the total collection, it is doubtful that the library was actively maintained after the turn of the century. This is also supported by Rampelmann's research:

> Although the *Turnverein* existed after the war, no new members were accepted into the club after 1918. As its members became older, it lost many of its gymnastic and social functions and, therefore, its importance in the community.[11]

Only two works, or 5.41%, were translations from English into German, one an autobiography of P. T. Barnum and the other a German translation of a Charles Dickens novel. German literature is the most dominant category, as with all other collections studied. Despite the small number of titles represented, there is an interesting overlap with other Turner library collections, as will be discussed later. Eleven of the 23 non-literature titles, or 47.83%, match non-literature titles owned by other Turner libraries studied. This figure would be even higher if only the authors of works were considered instead of the exact title. Most of the matches were in the areas of "History" and "Science."

Louisville Turngemeinde, Louisville, Kentucky. The 129 surviving volumes of the Louisville Turngemeinde library represent 36.9% of the possible 350 volumes reported to the national headquarters in 1920. The highest numbers of volumes reported were 600 in 1866 and 571 in 1914, but the collection was not stable:

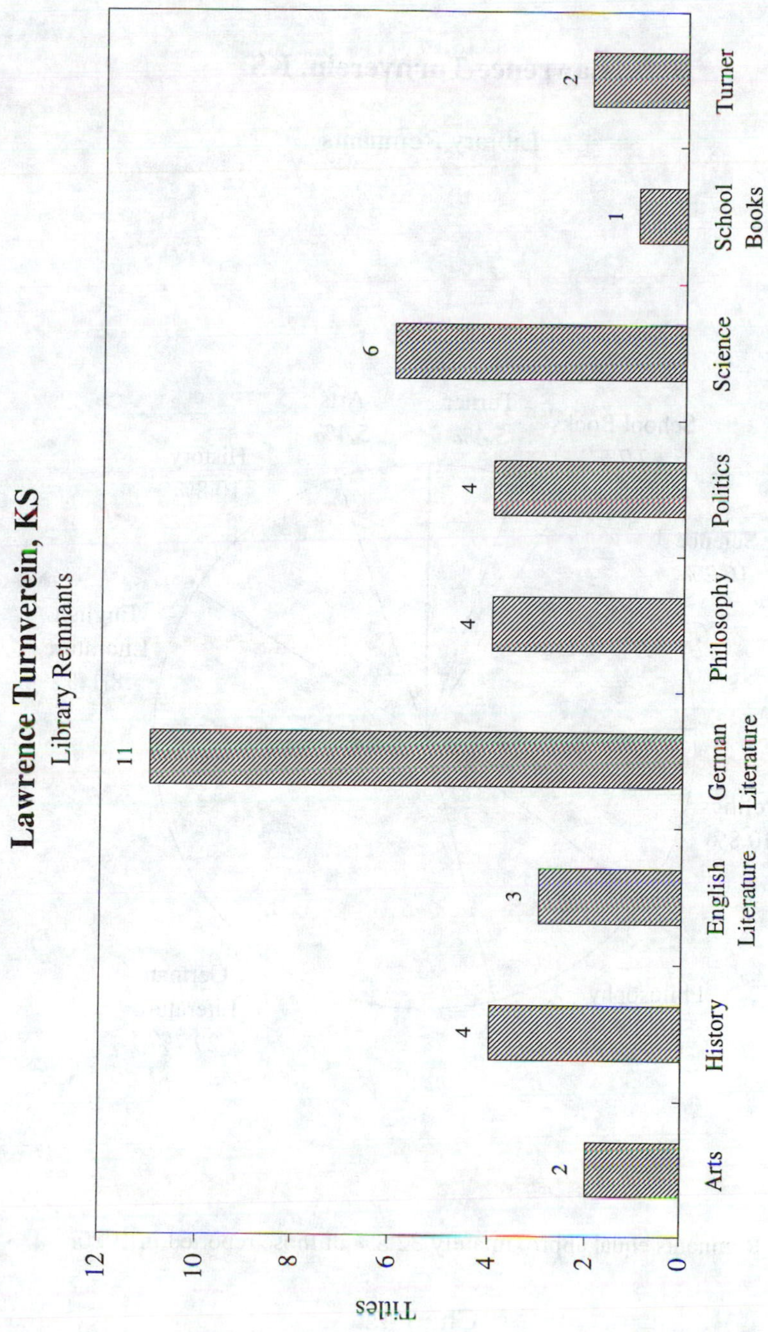
Lawrence Turnverein, KS
Library Remnants
Titles
0
2
4
6
8
10
12
Arts
History
English Literature
German Literature
Philosophy
Politics
Science
School Books
Turner
2
4
3
11
4
4
6
1
2

Chart 4.1

Lawrence Turnverein, KS

Library Remnants

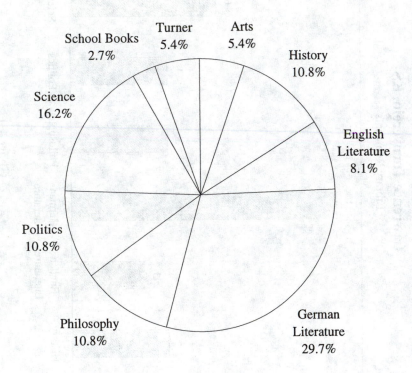

Remnants equal approximately 32.8% of those reported in 1920.

Chart 4.2

VOLUMES:	YEAR REPORTED:
600	1866
206	1890
500	1905
500	1910
571	1914
350	1920

It is not known why the number of volumes fluctuated so greatly. Charts 4.3 and 4.4 reflect the subject distribution of titles for the volumes remaining. Again, "German Literature" led all other categories of holdings. In terms of language of publication, German represented 77.97% of the collection with the remainder being English. Only ten titles were translations with six of these being translations of Dumas' novels into German. Dumas was one of the best represented French authors in the Turner collections. Two interesting translations from English into German were Edwin Freedley's *Der Geschäftsmann in Amerika* based on the author's *Treatise on Business* and George Napheys' *Das physische Leben des Weibes: Rathschläge für die Jungfrau, Gattin und Mutter*, translation of *The Physical Life of Women*. The former showed an interest in surviving within the American business world and was also owned by the St. Louis Public Library.

Seven of the 34 non-literature titles, or 20.59% matched similar holdings of other Turner libraries. These matches were distributed among five different categories. The two "History" matches were for Otto von Corvin's *Illustrirte Weltgeschichte für das Volk* and Gustav Struve's *Weltgeschichte*. Gustav Struve's work was the historical study most held by American Turner libraries although it was not held by either public library examined. The "Science" match was Humboldt's *Kosmos*, the most held scientific work among the Turner libraries and the public libraries. For the Louisville Turngemeinde the "Politics" category consisted only of United States government documents. This would have been very unusual since radical writers of the day were usually represented in Turner libraries, but it must be remembered that these volumes are only remnants. Other libraries examined confirm that such political writings probably did exist, particularly in the earlier years.

Aurora Turnverein, Chicago, Illinois. The Aurora Turnverein in Chicago, Illinois, was considered one of the most radical of the Turner organizations. Keil characterized the Aurora Turnverein as "the most important link between the

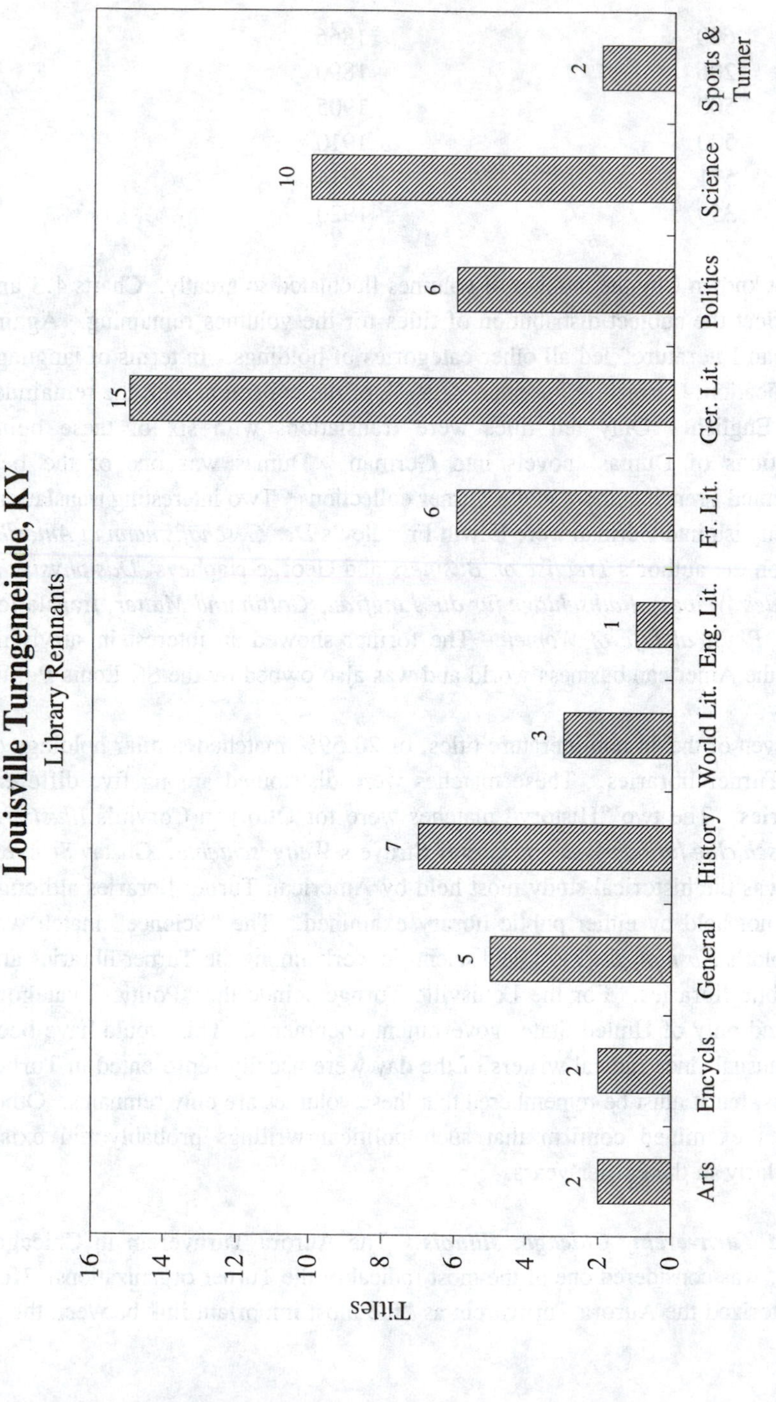
Louisville Turngemeinde, KY
Library Remnants
Titles
0
2
4
6
8
10
12
14
16
Arts
Encycls.
General
History
World Lit.
Eng. Lit.
Fr. Lit.
Ger. Lit.
Politics
Science
Sports & Turner
2
2
5
7
3
1
6
15
6
10
2

Chart 4.3

Louisville Turngemeinde, KY

Library Remnants

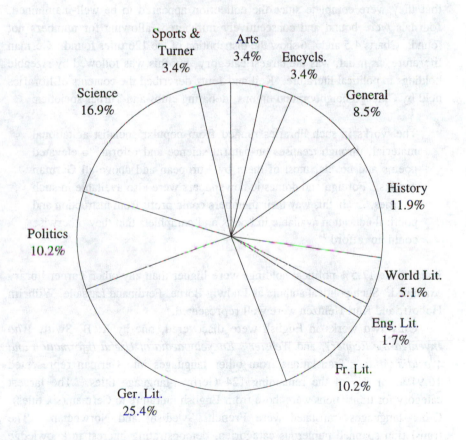

Remnants equal approximately 36.9% of vols. reported in 1920.
"Politics"category comprised only of GPO publications.

Chart 4.4

radical wing of the labor movement and the liberal middle class."[12] August Spies, hanged after the Haymarket Affair, was a prominent member of the Aurora Turnverein.[13] The remnants of the library collection reflect this orientation. Approximately 240 volumes, or 24%, of the 1,000 volumes reported to the national headquarters in 1920 were discovered by the researcher at the Illinois Turners Camp. The actual percentage reflected should probably be higher since many multi-volume sets were found with incomplete holdings, but only those volumes actually found were counted. In many instances it would be presumed that they were complete since the collection appeared to be well-maintained. Journals were bound and consecutively numbered, allowing for numbers not found. Charts 4.5 and 4.6 show the distribution of the 126 titles found. German literature, as usual, was the largest category, but this was followed by sizeable holdings in political literature. Keil and Jentz described the contents of libraries held by Chicago neighborhood unions, debating clubs and Turner societies:

> The works in such libraries ranged from popular socialist agitational material, through treatises on natural science and reform, to elevated poems and novels, most of them by European and above all German writers. Foreign and domestic newspapers were also available in such libraries. ... In this way their members could profit from instruction and political education available in books and pamphlets that they otherwise could not afford.[14]

Indeed, the 17.5% political holdings were higher than any other Turner library examined. Such political authors as Ludwig Börne, Ferdinand Lassalle, Wilhelm Hohoff, and Karl Heinzen were well represented.

Only two works in English were discovered, one by R. B. Swift, *Who Invented the Reaper?,* and *Webster's Encyclopaedia of Useful Information and World's Atlas*. Translations from other languages into German represented 16.94%, or 21, of the remaining 124 German-language titles. The largest category for translations were those from English literature to German (six titles). Other languages translated were French, Swedish, and Norwegian. The translation spanned numerous categories, demonstrating interest in knowledge from the world at-large. Of particular interest is Abbott's *Geschichte der Bürgerkrieges in Amerika*, published contemporarily during the Civil War with the English-language edition, *The History of the Civil War in America*. It contained a special introduction and *"Anhang"* for German-Americans.

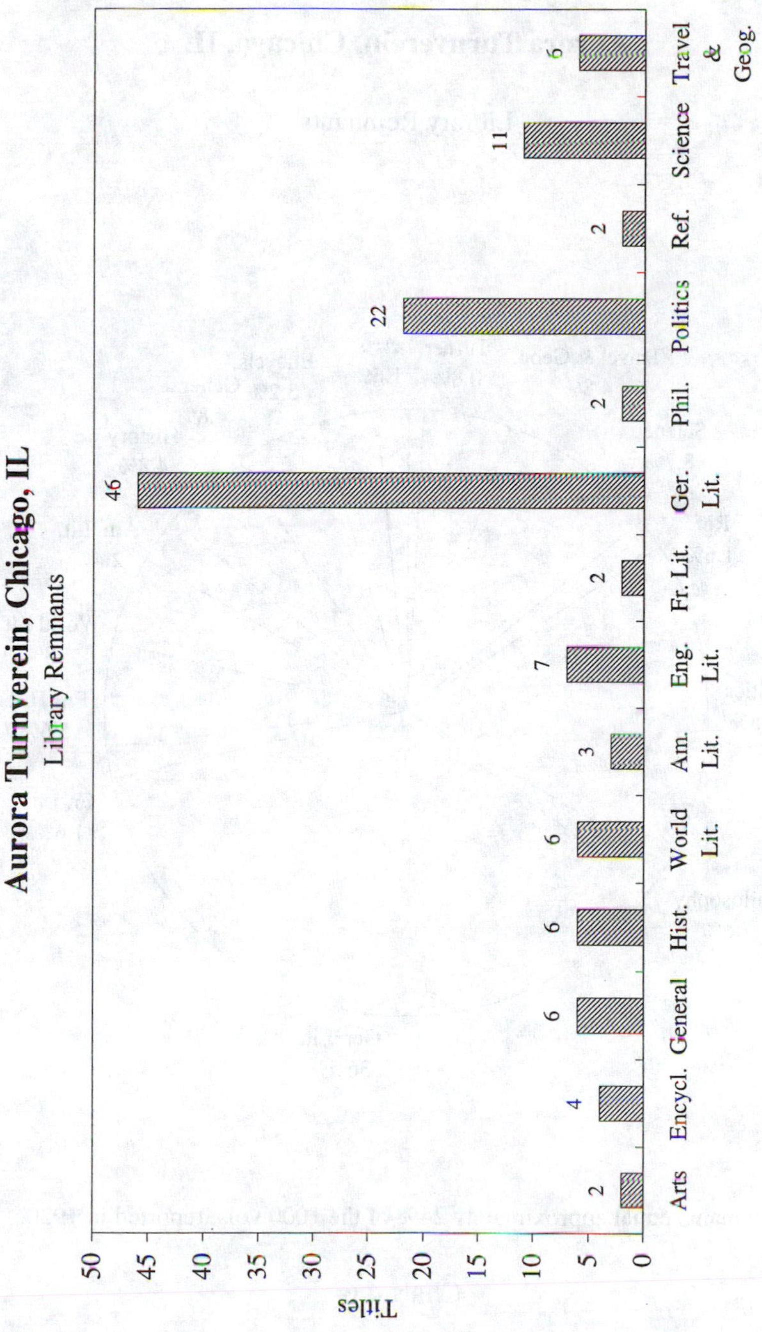

Aurora Turnverein, Chicago, IL
Library Remnants

Chart 4.5

Category	Titles
Arts	2
Encycl.	4
General	6
Hist.	6
World Lit.	6
Am. Lit.	3
Eng. Lit.	7
Fr. Lit.	2
Ger. Lit.	46
Phil.	2
Politics	22
Ref.	2
Science	11
Travel & Geog.	6

Aurora Turnverein, Chicago, IL

Library Remnants

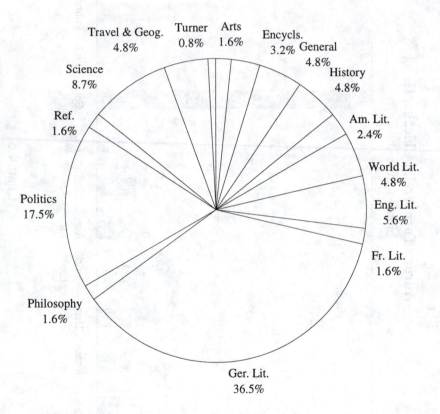

Remnants equal approximately 24% of the 1000 vols. reported in 1920.

Chart 4.6

Sixteen titles, or 25.81% of the non-literature portion of the collection, overlap with other Turner libraries under discussion. The highest overlap is in the area of general periodical titles (4), followed closely by "Science" (3) and "Politics" (3).

Milwaukee Turnverein, Milwaukee, Wisconsin. The Milwaukee Turnverein collection is now integrated with other German-American holdings in the Max Kade German-American Document & Research Center at the University of Kansas, Lawrence. The collection was originally given to the Milwaukee County Historical Museum in 1945[15] and was later removed to the Max Kade Center at Lawrence, Kansas. The individual titles belonging to the Milwaukee Turnverein were located by identifying those volumes with Milwaukee Turnverein book plates. Charts 4.7 and 4.8 show the distribution of subjects for those titles identified. Since the collection was not ordered in any way during examination, an attempt to count actual volumes was not practical. The 1914 statistics reported to the national headquarters were 6,400 volumes. However, only 448 titles were identified at Lawrence. Further evidence that these remnants do not represent the entire collection are provided by Walter Osten in his 1945 report to the Turners on the disposition of the library:

> One-third of the volumes are published in the English language. Among these English language volumes there is unfortunately not one single volume of literary value. Most of the volumes are handsomely bound volumes of U.S. Government reports, on the census, agriculture, education, commerce, laws, congressional, and senate records. These volumes, we can assure you, have never been opened or read. Besides these there is a 120 volume collection of the *War of the Rebellion*, and a 25 volume collection of the *Wisconsin Blue Books*, which evidently came from Emil Wallber's library. ... [One Turner] contributed a series of ten bound volumes of the *Boston Intelligencer*, a national Spiritualistic magazine.[16]

Since none of the above cited items were evident in the current collection, it must be assumed that the works were discarded or not passed on to Lawrence. Nevertheless, a few English-language publications were found. Three English-language publications were identified and one French, leaving 99.12% of the remnants in the German language. If Osten was correct, the remnants would reflect the most-used portion of the collection. Of the 448 titles, 68 titles, or 15.18%, were translations into German. These translations were primarily from

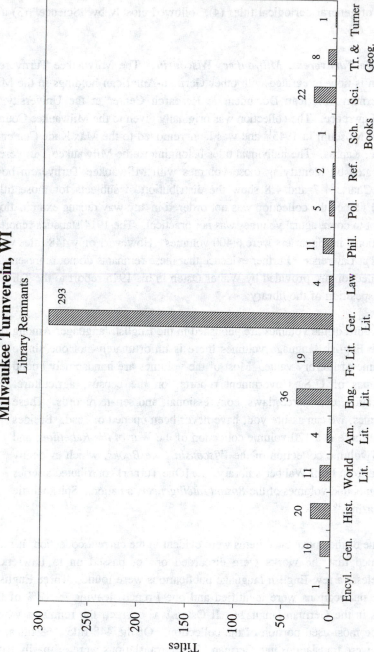

Milwaukee Turnverein, WI
Library Remnants

Chart 4.7

Milwaukee Turnverein, WI

Library Remnants

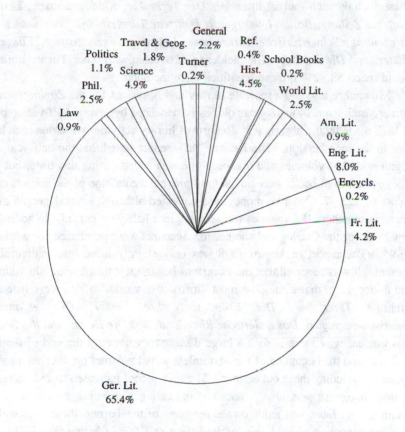

General 2.2%

Travel & Geog. 1.8%   Ref. 0.4%

Politics 1.1%   Turner 0.2%   School Books 0.2%

Science 4.9%   Hist. 4.5%

Phil. 2.5%   World Lit. 2.5%

Law 0.9%   Am. Lit. 0.9%

Eng. Lit. 8.0%

Encycls. 0.2%

Fr. Lit. 4.2%

Ger. Lit. 65.4%

Chart 4.8

French and English literary works. Fourteen journals and 434 monographic titles were identified. Of the non-literature category 45 titles out of 85, or 52.94%, matched other Turner library holdings in this study.

Receipts from bookstores and book-binders in the Turner collection of the Milwaukee County Historical Society also reflect that the collection was fairly well maintained.[17] In addition, subscriptions or bindery receipts for several periodical titles exist that either were not present in the titles listed in the Lawrence catalog, or did not have Milwaukee Turnverein ownership stamps. These include such journal titles as: *Der Techniker*, *Kladderadatsch*, *Leslie's Illustrirte Zeitung*, *Boston Investigator*, *Deutsche Turnzeitung*, *"Amerikanische" Turnzeitung*, *Schweizerische Turnzeitung*, *Deutsche Jugendzeitung*, *Fliegende Blätter*, and *Die Zukunft*. The incidence of overlap with other Turner libraries would reach 58.82% if these few titles were included.

Milwaukee also had a separate library and librarians for the *Zöglingsverein*, Turner youth from 14 to 18 years old, as is evidenced by several half-year reports in 1878 made by the librarians.[18] Reports of library activities were due each half-year to the membership. The January 1878 report stated that the half-year was begun with 294 volumes and that only one was added during this time, but that a large number of books were bound to improve the condition of the collection for a cost of $22.27. No fine money was collected although several people owed fines. Altogether, 188 volumes were loaned in a half-year period. In addition a new book for the Catalog and another for Accounts were purchased for a total of $0.95. The report in August 1878 was only slightly more informative about content. It was reported that the librarians began their terms with 206 volumes and added 18 to that sum. The most "instructive works" added were listed as: Brehm's *Thierleben*, *Die Erde und ihre Völker*, *Die gesammten Naturwissenschaften*, *Das malerische Rheinland*, and *Die Donau und ihr Gebiet*. It is unclear why there is such a large discrepancy between the end of the first half-year and the beginning of the next unless actual volumes on the shelves were counted, excluding those out on loan. The loan record increased to 281 volumes. A new bookcase was also purchased, indicating a growing collection. The Brehm's *Thierleben* was a title owned by many of the Turner libraries as well as both Indianapolis and St. Louis Public Libraries. *Die Erde und ihre Völker* and *Die gesammten Naturwissenschaften* both appear in the Lawrence catalog, but without the Milwaukee Turnverein ownership stamp. A number of school editions of titles also were in the catalog, which might indicate that some of the contents of the *Zöglingsverein*'s library were also donated although not containing the Milwaukee Turnverein ownership. This extremely brief view of the *Zöglingsverein* library did demonstrate the librarians' concern for purchasing instructive works, particularly in the sciences and travel and geography. A closer examination of these youth libraries would make an excellent case for further study, but documentation concerning these collections would probably prove even more elusive than that for the adult collections since little was discovered by the researcher to date.

Catalogs of Turner Libraries

Attention will now focus on Turner libraries which are represented here by catalogs: Wilmington Turngemeinde, St. Louis Turnverein, and Cincinnati Turngemeinde.

Wilmington Turngemeinde, Wilmington, Delaware. Although the Wilmington Turngemeinde catalog is undated, its entries correspond for the most part with the "Borrowers' Record Book" of that organization, covering dated entries from 1906 to 1932, so it might be assumed that the catalog was primarily accurate for that period. Undated entries come before those dated so they were probably from a slightly earlier period. Also, book remnants of the Wilmington Turngemeinde largely match those of the catalog with the major exception that more Turner publications were found. The latter publications were more likely part of the Turner office holdings rather than the library, if patterns of other Turner libraries are any indicators.

Charts 4.9 and 4.10 outline the general characteristics of the collection by categories. The contents of the Wilmington Turngemeinde is extensively covered in Chapter V, "Use," and will not be repeated here. The predominance of German literature for this collection is consistent with those of other Turner libraries. Seventeen out of 62 non-literature titles, or 27.52%, matched holdings of other Turnverein libraries.

St. Louis Turnverein, St. Louis, Missouri. The St. Louis Turnverein collection is represented by an 1895 catalog with handwritten additions. It is held in the Special Collections Department of the Library of Washington University, St. Louis, Missouri (Illustration 4.1). It appears to be the actual copy used by the Turnverein because of an ownership stamp as well as the existence of numbers on labels, matching those numbers in the catalog, which were laid between the pages of the catalog as if to be used on the books when the items were entered in the catalog. A large proportion of book numbers have been crossed off and new numbers reassigned. The printed portion of the catalog contained just book numbers, but handwritten corrections apparently assigned symbols and new numbers for other than German novels. It is unknown how long this catalog with

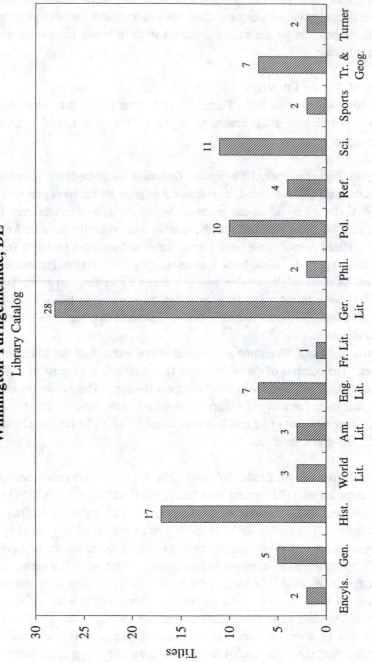

Wilmington Turngemeinde, DE
Library Catalog

Chart 4.9

Wilmington Turngemeinde, DE

Library Catalog

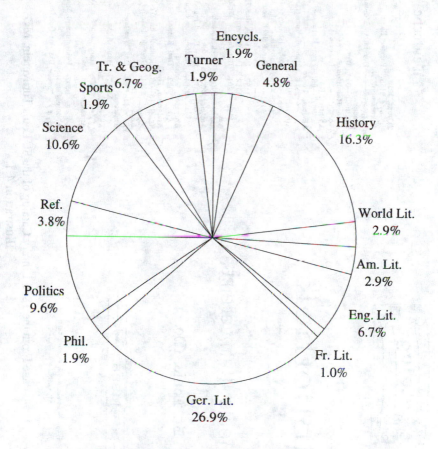

Chart 4.10

Deutsche Werke.

About, Edw. Pariser Ehen.
    Eng 2155.
    405-6 178-9. Der letzte Monmorency.   2 Bde.
Ackermann, W.
Aeschylos. Werke.   2 "
    Spe 2601—02.
Aide, Hamilton.
    Eng 2257—58. Imogen.   2 "
Ahlgren, E.
    Spe 2697—98. Frau Marianne.   2 "
Alarcon, Pedro A. de.
    Spe 2514. Manuel Venegras.
Alexis, Willibert.
    1184—88. Ruhe ist die erste Bürgerpflicht.   5 "
    1189—90. Cabanis.   2 "
    1191—93. Der Roland von Berlin.   3 "
    1194—96. Isegrim.   3 "
    1197. Die Hosen des Herrn von Bredow.
    1198. Der Wärwolf.
    1199 —1201. Der falsche Woldemar.   3 "
Am. 2700. Glück vorbei.
Amicis, Edurondo de.
    Spd 2372. Eine Schultragödie.
    Spd 2584. Skizzen aus dem Soldatenleben.
Amyntor, Gerhard v.
    Spe 2632. Drei Küsse.
Anderson, H. C.
    Fr 1610—13. Sämmtliche Werke.   4 "
    Spe 2261. Geschichten.   4246—7
Andree, Dr. Carl.
    340 356 Das Westland.
Andree.
    X. 57. Hand-Atlas.   2 "
Angerstein, Ed.
    45/4 777. Handbuch für Turner.
Ansongruber, Ludw.
    Rt 1690—99. Werke.   10 "
Apostelgeschichte,
    2507. Feldrain und Waldweg.
    965 Die des Geistes.

Katalog

—der—

Bibliothek

—des—

St. Louis Turnvereins,

St. Louis, Mo.

1895.

Aug. Wiebuch & Son Printing Co.,
ST. LOUIS, MO.

Page From the 1895 Library Catalog of the St. Louis Turnverein, MO

Illustration 4.1

the handwritten additions may have served as the main catalog. There were 1,646 titles identified, including the additions. The following statistics were reported to the national headquarters for library holdings:

LIBRARY HOLDINGS	YEAR REPORTED
2,955 vols.	1895
4,000 vols.	1900
3,500 vols.	1905
5,000 vols.	1910
5,000 vols.	1914
3,000 vols.	1920

The catalog is divided into *Deutsche Werke* and *Englische Werke*. No other languages are represented although there are a number of translations from English and French into German, especially for literary works. German-language materials far outweigh those in English for every category including American and English literature. Charts 4.11 and 4.12 show the graphic distribution of subject categories for this library. The count of titles includes both English and German works and those which were handwritten additions. Literature, especially German literature, overwhelms holdings for other categories with a combined total of 79.7% of the collection.

The percentage of the collection devoted to "Science" (3.1%) was unusually low compared to the other Turner libraries studied. Normally the "Science" percentage ranked among the top five categories. However, an excellent collection of works in this area was held by a nearby library, that of the St. Louis Deutsches Institut für Wissenschaft, Kunst und Gewerbe, founded in 1856, only six years after the founding of the St. Louis Turnverein.[19] Since German was the main language of that collection also, there may have been little cause to compete in these subject areas of science, business, and industry. One did have to be a member of the Deutsches Institut to use its library, but friends of members, when accompanied by the member, could also use the reading room and library. The reading room was open every day, except for three holidays, from 9 a.m. to 10 p.m. so there was ample access to the collection.[20] The holdings of its 1860 catalog confirm a similar scientific world outlook to that of the Turners. Indeed, the *Turn-Zeitung*, 1857–60, was listed as one of its journal holdings. Even in 1860 the catalog listed many contemporarily published titles, and 70 journal titles recorded were published worldwide from such places as Paris, Berlin, Leipzig, Boston, New York City, Cincinnati, Milwaukee, London, and Vienna. Holdings

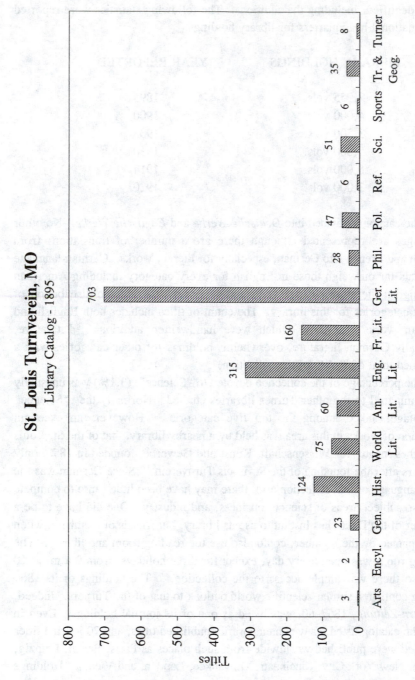

St. Louis Turnverein, MO

Library Catalog - 1895

Chart 4.11

St. Louis Turnverein, MO

Library Catalog - 1895

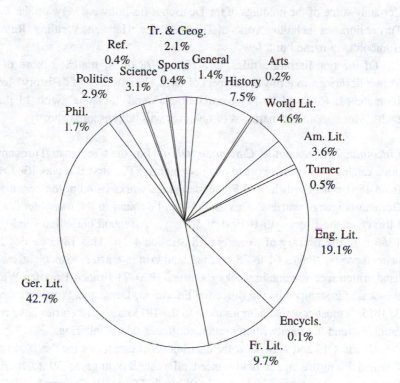

Ref.
0.4%

Tr. & Geog.
2.1%

Sports
0.4%

Science
3.1%

Politics
2.9%

General
1.4%

Arts
0.2%

History
7.5%

Phil.
1.7%

World Lit.
4.6%

Am. Lit.
3.6%

Turner
0.5%

Eng. Lit.
19.1%

Ger. Lit.
42.7%

Encycls.
0.1%

Fr. Lit.
9.7%

Includes handwritten additions.

Chart 4.12

of both monographs and journals were in German, English, and French with German predominating. The stated purpose of the Deutsches Institut certainly conforms to Turner principles:

> Der Zweck des Instituts ist, die Mittel zur Erlangung von Kentnissen in allen Zweigen von Wissenschaft, Kunst und Gewerbe möglichst allgemein zugänglich zu machen und dadurch die wissenschaftliche Bildung under den Deutschen in St. Louis zu förden.[21]

Certainly some of the holdings of the Deutsches Institut were very similar to other Turner libraries including works of Thomas Paine, Heinzen, Weitling, Ritter, and Humboldt, to name but a few.

Of the non-literature titles, 24.42%, or 78 titles, matched those of other Turner libraries. In terms of numbers of titles, the category of "History" led with 16 matches, followed by "General/Journals" and "Science" with 14 matches each. More about comparisons of holdings will be presented shortly.

Cincinnati Turngemeinde, Cincinnati, Ohio. For the Cincinnati Turngemeinde three catalog "versions" exist in two documents. The first is a classified catalog from 1861 with English- and French-language works listed at the conclusion of German-language entries. This catalog can be found in the pamphlet file at the Library of the Cincinnati Historical Society. A second classified catalog from 1866 is in the Library of Congress (Illustration 4.2). This 1866 catalog has 60 printed pages. Pages 61 to 75 contain handwritten entries. Since entries in the handwritten section contain works about the 1870–71 Franco-Prussian War, and the catalog is stamped by the Bureau of Education, Department of Interior on July 3, 1875, it must contain additions close to the 1875 date. All entries have running numbers, and the handwritten section continues this numbering.

Charts 4.13 and 4.14 show the distribution of categories for the 1861 catalog. German literature again outdistanced all other holdings at 39.2%. English literature was the second highest at 11.0% with "Travel & Geography" following at 9.0%. Chart 4.15 shows the change in proportions compared to the printed portion of the 1866 catalog. The German literature section grew disproportionately, now represented by 61.8% of the holdings. The second largest category now switches to "History" at 7.0% with "Travel & Geography" remaining third at 6.0%. Chart 4.16 is a comparison of the catalogs for 1861, 1866, and 1866 with additions. Obviously, "German Literature" continued to lead titles added to the collection. There was a 200.3% increase in German literature by 1866 and an additional 20% increase thereafter. Other substantial

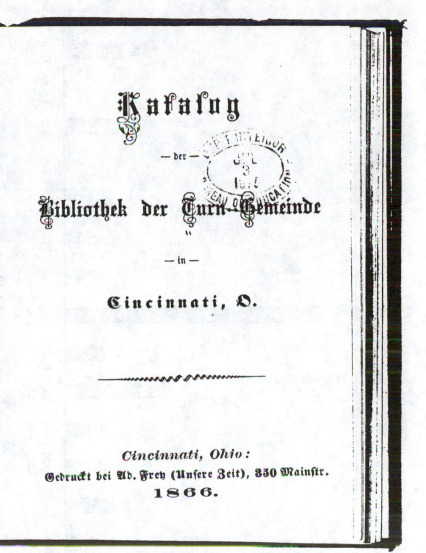

Title Page of the 1866 Library Catalog of the Cincinnati
Turngemeinde, OH

Illustration 4.2

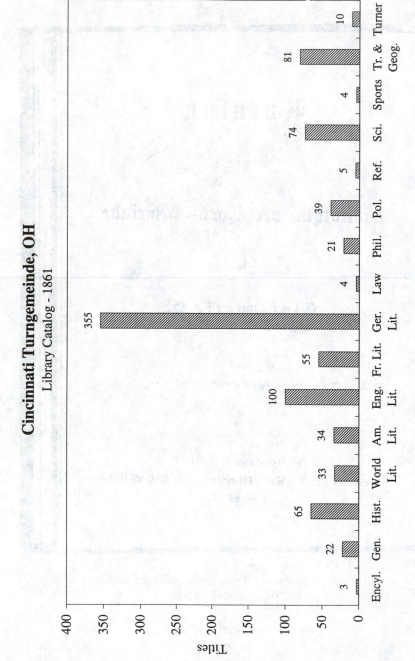

Cincinnati Turngemeinde, OH
Library Catalog - 1861

Chart 4.13

Cincinnati Turngemeinde, OH

Library Catalog - 1861

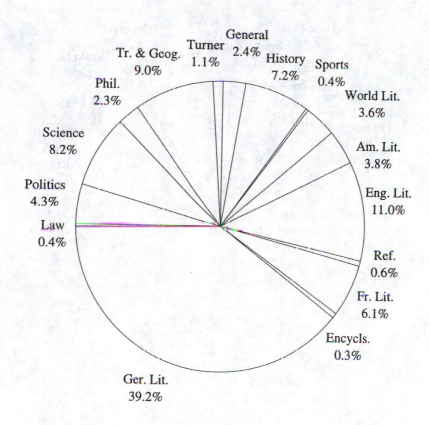

General 2.4%

Turner 1.1%

Tr. & Geog. 9.0%

History 7.2%

Sports 0.4%

Phil. 2.3%

World Lit. 3.6%

Science 8.2%

Am. Lit. 3.8%

Politics 4.3%

Eng. Lit. 11.0%

Law 0.4%

Ref. 0.6%

Fr. Lit. 6.1%

Encycls. 0.3%

Ger. Lit. 39.2%

Chart 4.14

Cincinnati Turngemeinde, OH

Library Catalog - 1866

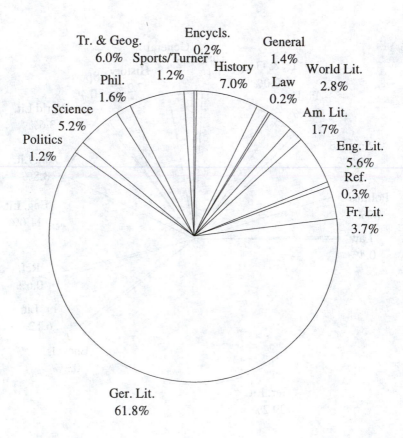

Excludes about 300 GPO and 20 French volumes.

Chart 4.15

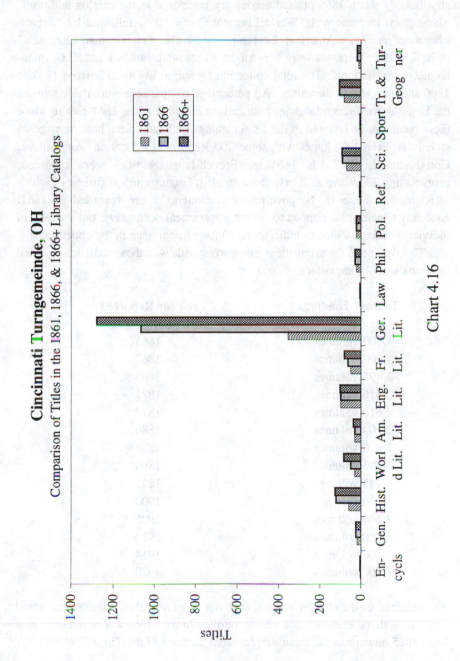

Cincinnati Turngemeinde, OH

Comparison of Titles in the 1861, 1866, & 1866+ Library Catalogs

Chart 4.16

increases from 1861 to 1866 were "History" at 105.1%, "Turner" at 70%, and "Philosophy" at 35%. However, most of the categories do not increase significantly when 1866 printed entries are compared to the catalog additions. The highest increase was "World Literature" at 67.3%, followed by "French Literature" at 27%, "American Literature" at 24.1%, and "German Literature" at 20%. Other increases were very slight. These latter titles were all German-language translations. The total collection increased by 102.3% from 1861 to 1866 and only 16.3% thereafter. All percentage comparisons were made without the English- and French-language publications included in the 1861 catalog since these could not be counted in the 1866 catalog. A handwritten note on page 75 stated "20 French Volumes with some 300 Reports of Education, Agriculture, Congressional, etc." In 1861 ten French-language titles were recorded, representing 13 volumes. Forty-three English-language titles, fifteen of which were multi-volume U. S. government documents, were recorded in 1861. Evidently Cincinnati continued to collect government documents, but the lack of individual listings seems to indicate their lesser importance in the collection.

This decline in the acquisitions rate corresponds with those statistics reported to the national headquarters:

Library Holdings	Year Reported
3,700 volumes	1866
5,000 volumes	1867
2,495 volumes	1869
2,516 volumes	1871
2,610 volumes	1872
2,500 volumes	1880
2,600 volumes	1885
2,793 volumes	1890
2,745 volumes	1895
3,000 volumes	1900
3,560 volumes	1905
2,500 volumes	1910
1,500 volumes	1914
1,500 volumes	1920

As discussed in the chapter on use, it is not surprising that acquisitions would diminish with the existence of a nearby public library which was actively buying from 1865 onward in the same subject areas as those of the Turner collection.

Publication dates are not included in the catalogs, and it would be impossible to verify with certainty which editions of a title were held without the volumes themselves. However, dates for journal holdings were usually given, as well as indications of which titles were on subscription. Many of the journal titles listed in the 1861 catalog may have been gifts since 19 of the 27 titles do not have holdings beyond 1859. However, more extensive study would be needed to verify this since one such title, *Volks-Tribun*, a labor press publication, was only produced in 1846,[22] and *Der Erzähler am Ohio* was published from 1849–1850,[23] according to Cazden. Thus, the lack of continued holdings for some titles have been because of the nature of publication rather than due to a lack of interest in procurement. The seven titles listed as under subscription were *Die Fackel*, *Fliegende Blätter*, *Gartenlaube*, *Novellen-Zeitung*, *Unterhaltungen am häuslichen Heerde*, *Polytechnisches Centralblatt*, and *Die Natur*. Five of these titles overlapped with other Turner libraries. By 1866 thirty journal titles were listed, but only five were listed as subscriptions: *Gartenlaube* (Leipzig), *Gerhard's Deutsch-Amerikanische Gartenlaube*, *Die Deutsch-Amerikanischen Monatshefte* (Chicago), *Leipziger Illustrirte Zeitung*, and *Polytechnisches Centralblatt*. Only two titles remained on continuing subscription from 1861. All four of the first titles listed overlapped with several other Turner libraries. Four of the titles not on subscription had volumes added to the original number given in 1861, and five titles were new to the list, including the newer subscription titles listed above. Some volumes were no longer listed or were marked "fehlt."

Of the composite titles, only 14.72% of its 428 non-literature entries matched those of other Turner libraries. "History" and "Science" equally out-paced other categories in matches, followed by "General/Journals" and "Philosophy." The Cincinnati Turner library had the lowest percentage overlap of non-literature titles of all Turner libraries examined even though the number of titles held in the non-literature categories was very similar to those held by the St. Louis Turnverein, another major library. One reason for this could have been the surprisingly small increase in non-literature titles after 1866. Only eight titles were added to the non-literature categories of the 1866 catalog if the hand-written additions are accurate. This does not include United States government document titles. Holdings for other Turner libraries under scrutiny, including remnants, held a greater percentage of non-literature titles with later publication dates. However, a large number of matches in many categories pre-dated 1871.

German-Language Holdings of Public Libraries

Two German-language collections of public libraries were included in this study in order to compare holdings. Only the German-language titles were included since the above contents analysis showed that the Turner libraries were composed primarily of works in German. Two such contemporary catalogs for public libraries were located for the St. Louis Public Library and the Indianapolis Public Library. Both were cities in which Turner libraries were also located, and both had separately published catalogs for German works. Some loan statistics were also available for these locations as is discussed in the chapter on usage. This confirms that these collections were actively used by the communities involved. Was the content of these public library German collections similar to those of the Turner libraries? Did the public library serve a similar purpose for the German-American community as the Turner library based on content?

Indianapolis Public Library, Indianapolis, Indiana. Two catalogs of the German-language collection for the Indianapolis Public Library survived.[24] One from 1893 was used for this study since it was more inclusive. Charts 4.17 and 4.18 give the distribution by subject according to the categories established for examination of the Turner collections. The distribution of the 1,287 titles is remarkably similar to those of the Turner libraries, particularly in the dominance of German literature at 74.8% of the collection. "English Literature," "History," and "Science" achieved the next highest rankings in that order. These categories also were consistently among the top five categories by percentage for the Turner libraries. Further information on the collection will be presented with the comparison study.

St. Louis Public Library, St. Louis, Missouri. The 1880 catalog of the St. Louis Public Library is actually that of the St. Louis Public School Library, the precursor to the public library (Illustration 4.3).[25] At the time of the catalog there was a small subscription fee for use of the library, but eligibility was open to the whole community. The German collection was very substantial with 2,251 titles identified in the catalog. Many sets of works are included in this number, so the total holdings are very impressive. Consistent with other counts, titles cataloged as sets were counted as one title even if analytics were provided. The juvenile section of the classified catalog was not included in the category count since that was not a focus of any of the other collections. Another category which did not coincide with any other collections was that of "Library Science." These 25 titles were included separately in the count since they were adult literature. Charts 4.19 and 4.20 represent the subject distribution found. Once again, German literature surpassed other categories at 36.1%, but not to the extreme found in the Indianapolis Public Library or in many of the Turner libraries. "Science" was a very strong second in terms of percentages with 21.6%. St. Louis was a major

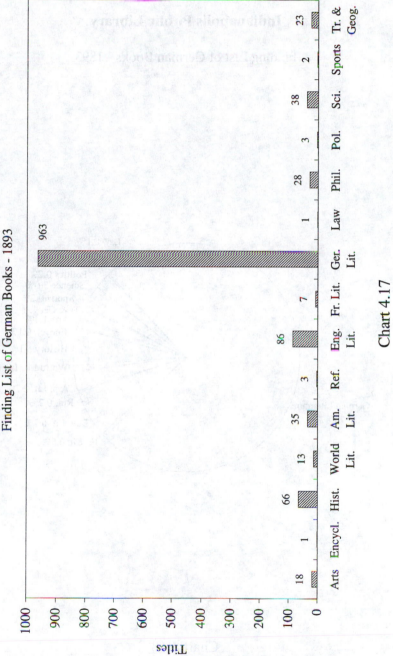

Indianapolis Public Library
Finding List of German Books - 1893

Chart 4.17

Indianapolis Public Library

Finding List of German Books - 1893

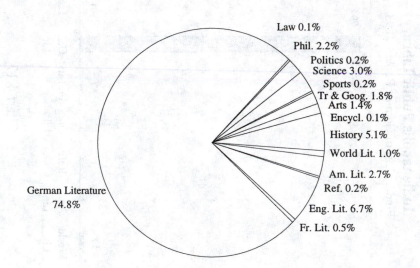

Law 0.1%

Phil. 2.2%

Politics 0.2%
Science 3.0%

Sports 0.2%
Tr & Geog. 1.8%
Arts 1.4%

Encycl. 0.1%

History 5.1%

World Lit. 1.0%

Am. Lit. 2.7%
Ref. 0.2%

Eng. Lit. 6.7%

Fr. Lit. 0.5%

German Literature
74.8%

Chart 4.18

KLASSIFICIRTER

KATALOG.

NEBST ALPHABETISCHEM REGISTER

DER DEUTSCHEN WERKE

BIBLIOTHEK DER ÖFFENTLICHEN SCHULEN

VON ST. LOUIS.

14949

DECEMBER, 1880.

SYSTEM DER KLASSIFICATION.

Die drei Hauptabtheilung. Kataloge sind :WISSENSCHAFT, KUNST u. GESCHICHTE

Diese vertheilen sich in hundert Klassen und Unter-Klassen wie folgt:

1. WISSENSCHAFT.

2-5. Philosophie.
6-16. Theologie.
17-31. Staatswissenschaften und Erziehungswesen.

61. KUNST.

62. Romanliteratur.
65-68. Schöne Künste und Poesie.
70. Jugendschriften.
71-78. Literaturgeschichte und vermischte Schriften.

79. GESCHICHTE.

80-87. Geographie; Reisebeschreibungen.
88-96. Historische Werke.
97. Biographie.

ANHANG.

98.
99. Encyklopädien.
100. Zeitschriften.

DIE EINRICHTUNG DES KATALOGS.

Um das Nachschlagen zu erleichtern, sind über etliche allgemeine Regeln angegeben welche dem Leser als Führer dienen sollen. Das Verzeichniss eines Werkes ist entweder unter dem Namen des Verfassers, seines Pseudonyms (fingirten Namens), oder unter dem Worte Titel zu finden, und wird vor dem bekanntesten Namen der Hauptgebraucht mache. Anonyme Werke sind unter dem ersten Wort des Titels verzeichnet, mit Ausnahme des Artikels. Sammlungen sind unter dem Namen des Herausgebers verzeichnet. Novellen und Jugendschriften sind unter dem Autor, oder unter dem Titel zu finden. Die fett Schrift gibt das Hauptverzeichnis des Werkes sowie ein Klassennummer an und bestimmt den Platz, welchen das Buch auf dem Bücherbrett einnimmt.

BEDINGUNGEN DER MITGLIEDSCHAFT.

Das vierunmatliche Abonnement beträgt $1.00. Die Lebensmitgliedschaft kostet $25. In jährlichen Beiträgen von $0.25 zahlbar. Nur Bewohner der Stadt sind zur Mitgliedschaft unter obigen Bedingungen berechtigt.

Mitglieder werden gebeten, die Verwaltung der Bibliothek von unvollständigen Büchern in Kenntnis zu setzen, damit dieselben durch vollständige ersetzt werden können.

DAS BULLETIN DER ÖFFENTLICHEN BIBLIOTHEK

wird publizirt um den Mitgliedern Nachricht von den neuen, der Bibliothek einverleibte Werken zu geben, und ihnen in der Auswahl der Bücher behülflich zu sein. Durch es als ein Theil desselben nur kaum dieser deutsche Katalog gedruckt werden, und sollte es ad Unterwaltung der Mitglieder erhalten, so werden noch andere Klassenlisten im Druck erscheinen. Die Einzelnummer des Bulletin kostet 10 Cents. Der jährliche Subscriptions preis der sechs Nummern beträgt 60 Cents, für welchen dasselbe an Abonnenten postfrei versandt wird.

Die Bibliotheksverwaltung giebt das Bulletin zu dem Zwecke heraus, den Mitgliedern sowie dem Publicum jede Hülfe und Bequemlichkeit zu sichern, welche die Mittel der Bibliothek erlauben. Hülfschläge in Bezug auf alle Bibliotheksangelegenheiten werden gern entgegengenommen werden. Man beliebe zu addressieren an

F. M. CRUNDEN, *Bibliothekar.*

Illustration 4.3: Pages From the 1880 Library Catalog of the St. Louis Public School Library (later St. Louis Public Library)

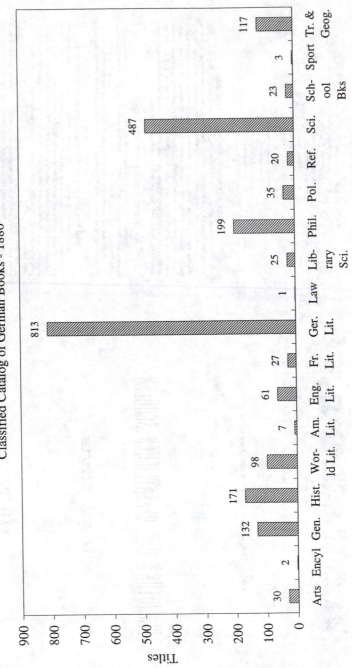

St. Louis Public Library

Classified Catalog of German Books - 1880

Chart 4.19

St. Louis Public Library

Classified Catalog of German Books - 1880

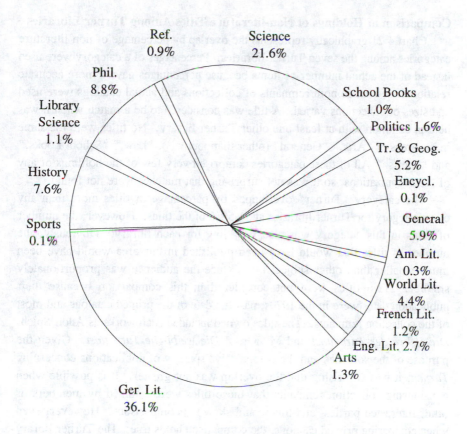

Ref.
0.9%

Science
21.6%

Phil.
8.8%

School Books
1.0%

Library
Science
1.1%

Politics 1.6%

Tr. & Geog.
5.2%

History
7.6%

Encycl.
0.1%

General
5.9%

Sports
0.1%

Am. Lit.
0.3%

World Lit.
4.4%

French Lit.
1.2%

Eng. Lit. 2.7%

Arts
1.3%

Ger. Lit.
36.1%

One book of law -- less than 0.1% not included.

Chart 4.20

regional center of business and industry, which may help explain the emphasis. The next highest category of "Philosophy" was some distance back at 8.8%. "Philosophy" did not fall into the top five categories of the Turner libraries, except once. The next category of "History" at 7.6% placed in the top five of Turner libraries, but the following one of "General" at 5.9% did not. Thus, the general percentage distribution does not seem to follow strongly the patterns established by the Turner libraries except for "German Literature." Further comparison of categories and holdings follows.

Comparison of Holdings of Non-literature Titles Among Turner Libraries

Chart 4.21 graphically represents the overlap by percentage of non-literature categories among the seven Turner libraries. Percentages of a category were used instead of the actual number of items because percentages gave a more accurate relational view since both remnants of collections and actual catalogs were used and sizes of collections varied. A title was considered to be a match when it was held in common with at least one other Turner library. No titles were the same in the areas of "Arts," "General" (other than journals), "Law," "School Books," and "Sports." All of these categories comprised very few of the holdings of any of the organizations, so it was not surprising that matches were not found.

The category "Turner" overlapped by percentage of titles more than any other category for Turner libraries at 31.58% of the titles. However, the number of titles in this category was also very low for each library. Obviously, the number of titles that would have been published in this area would have been much smaller than other subject areas since the audience was proportionately smaller. Two titles were not considered in this comparison because their publication dates were in the 1920s, past the date of the printed catalogs and most of the collection remnants. The titles owned included such works as Adolf Spieß' *Die Lehre der Turnkunst* and M. Kloss' *Die weibliche Turnkunst*. Given the purpose of the societies and the comparative sparsity of publications concerning *Turnen*, it was surprising that the overlap was not greater. It is possible when considering collection remnants that these titles were retained by members or other interested parties, and this would skew the comparisons. However, even when comparing printed catalogs, the comparison holds true. The Turner library with the greatest number of publications related to *Turnen*, was Cincinnati. When the Cincinnati Turngemeinde printed catalog was compared to the St. Louis Turnverein catalog, only two titles in this category matched. The small percentage of the collections represented by *Turnen* suggests that this was not a major focus of the Turner libraries despite the fact that gymnastics was a major purpose of the organizations. A few of the health titles related to anatomy,

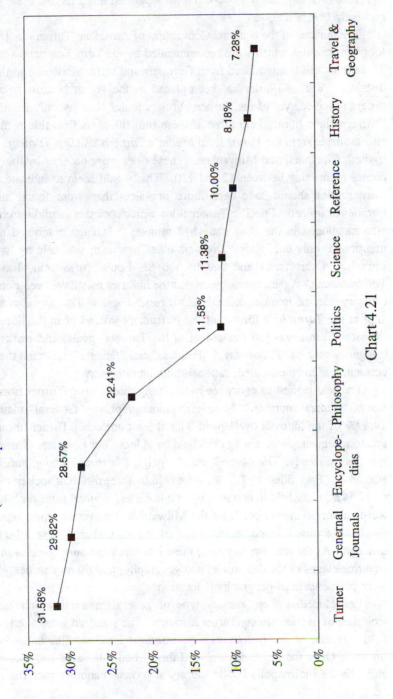

Overlap Among Turnverein Libraries by Category
(No overlap for: Arts, General, Law, School Books, Sports)

Chart 4.21

categorized under "Science," would have supported this area, but these were also relatively few in number.

The minutes of the National Convention of American Turners in 1866 listed four Turner titles which were recommended by the Turn Teachers' Congress.[26] These titles had been ordered from Germany and were distributed to the Turner districts. A second order had been placed by the *Vorort* because of additional orders received, yet of the Turner libraries under scrutiny only the Cincinnati Turngemeinde library held three of these four titles. A fifth title mentioned as also available from the *Vorort*,[27] Ed Müller's *Turnerbook* (*Das Turnen*), was held by both Cincinnati and Milwaukee. These titles were ordered by the *Vorort* in copies numbering between 12 and 110. This would seem to indicate that such Turner titles should have been more prevalent than were found among the libraries examined. Specific Turner titles which societies should purchase were also mentioned in the 1868 and 1872 minutes.[28] Of the combined nine titles mentioned, only one, Kloss' *Die weibliche Turnkunst*, was held by two Turner libraries in this study and one by the St. Louis Turnverein, Ravenstein's *Volksturnbuch*. Again, one suspects that the libraries may have been richer in this category than the remnant collections suggest. These works may also have been kept at the *Turnschule* for use of the instructors instead of in the library itself. Physical fitness was just one aspect of the Turners' goals, and works in other categories such as "Philosophy," "Politics," and "Science" reflected the Turners commitment to an educated, rational-thinking citizenry.

The next highest category for overlapping titles among Turner libraries was that of "General Journals." None of the monographs in "General" matched, but 29.82% of the journals overlapped with at least one other Turner library. The greatest frequency was among titles held by at least four libraries. Three journals met this frequency: *Die Gartenlaube* (Leipzig), *Illustrirte Zeitung*, and *Vom Fels zum Meer*. Four titles, or 7.02%, were held by three different societies; 10 titles, or 17.54%, were held in common by two libraries. Journal titles for which there were subscription receipts from the Milwaukee Turnverein, mentioned above, would have raised the percentage of overlap even higher if these titles had been included. As the category suggests, these journals were fairly general in content, covering events of the day, travel and geography, and literary pieces. Holdings were independent of geographical location.

Encyclopedias were another type of general material which had a high incidence of overlap among Turner libraries. The standard general encyclopedia held was that of the *Brockhaus Conversations Lexikon*, although others were owned. Only the St. Louis Public Library had this same encyclopedia title, although the Indianapolis Public Library also owned another such title.

"Philosophy" titles overlapped by 22.41%. Within this category were works by many religious and philosophical "radicals" who stressed religious liberalism, often in the form of *Freie Gemeinde* (Free Societies or Congregations), or liberal-thinking Christians, as well as works of moral deists, and anti-clerical authors.[29] Such titles included Gustav Wislicenus' *Die Bibel für denkende Leser betrachtet*, Franz Schmidt's *Heimkehr vom Himmel zur Erde*, Thomas Paine's *Theologische Werke*, Georg Korn's *Katechismus des Kulturmenschen* and Ludwig Büchner's *Natur und Geist*. The latter could also conceivably be listed under "Science." Many of the placements were made according to the categories the Turners themselves chose. Information about the Greek and Roman myths and philosophy was also placed here. This philosophical collection was definitely liberal in character.

"Politics" as a category was also radically oriented. Titles which overlapped decidedly reflected this orientation: Weitling's *Harmonie und Freiheit*, several of Max Nordau's works such as, *Die Krankheit des Jahrhunderts*, several of Karl Heinzen's works, August Bebel's *Die Frau und der Sozialismus*, Ferdinand Lassalle's *Macht und Recht*, etc.

"Science" titles again reflected a secular view. Popular, rationalistic science works were prominent in Turner collections. Such works supported the world outlook of the Turners. The most owned title of any category, with one exception, was Humboldt's *Kosmos*. This work was held in five of the seven Turner libraries. Other scientists following Humboldt's example were Emil Rossmässler, Hermann Burmeister, and Karl Vogt,[30] all of whom were well-represented in Turner libraries. Cazden described the works of Karl Vogt, Jacob Moleschott, and Ludwig Büchner as scientific materialists.[31] These authors were likewise strongly represented in the scientific works held. Büchner's *Kraft und Stoff* was one of the most held titles after Humboldt's *Kosmos*. One other title in "Science" overlapped equally with Büchner, *Buch der Erfindungen, Gewerbe und Industrien* (Book of Inventions, Business and Industry). This multi-volume set or its successor, *Neue Buch der Erfindungen* ..., was also held by four Turner libraries.

The categories of "Turner," "Philosophy," "Politics," and "Science" all reflected the same rationalistic, "radical" outlook in content and were the non-literature categories most overlapped among Turner libraries. A number of these titles were also mentioned in the 1866 minutes as being held by the national headquarters.[32]

"History" titles showed greater variation among the libraries, but certain authors associated with the Forty-Eighters or liberal viewpoints were among those that matched most. Gustav Struve's *Weltgeschichte* equalled Humboldt's *Kosmos* as owned by the most libraries, five out of seven. Some interest in the affairs of Germany remained since the work, *Der deutsch-französische Krieg, herausgegeben von Generalstab*, was held by four libraries along with non-matching, other works about the Franco-Prussian War. However, a definite interest in biographies about Americans and American history was evident. There were many different histories of the United States, whether translated into or written in German, but a German translation of George Bancroft's *Geschichte der Vereinigten Staaten* overlapped in several Turner libraries. History contained more English-language titles than other non-literature categories. These titles entailed American history topics, demonstrating an interest in the adopted homeland whether in German or English.

Titles in "Travel & Geography" matched least among Turner libraries. These titles were less politically oriented and reflected an interest in a broad range of geographical locations. Most of the titles were in German, but translations from a variety of languages were included.

The average percentage overlap of all non-literature categories was 30.53%. Although there was great similarity in the type of liberal authors chosen, the actual titles held were significantly different.

Comparison With the German Collections of Two Public Libraries

As was demonstrated above, the holdings of the two public libraries' German-language collections, Indianapolis Public Library and St. Louis Public Library, were very similar in proportion to those of the Turner libraries. However, a closer examination is needed to discover if the titles offered would have served the same purpose for the Turner communities as those in their own libraries. Again, the non-literature categories were compared since they more strongly coincide with the stated purpose of the organizations.

Chart 4.22 gives the percentage of overlap between these two German-language public library collections and the collections of the seven Turner libraries. The English-language titles of the Turner libraries were not included in this percentage since the public library catalogs do not reflect this aspect. Since the English-language sections of Turner libraries were proportionally so small, and many of the English-language titles were literature, this will not affect the comparison significantly. For comparison Chart 4.23 plots the percentage of overlap by category among Turner libraries and between the seven Turner libraries and the two public libraries.

"General/Journals" matched by 15 out of 54 titles, or 27.78%, reflecting the highest overlap in terms of percentage of a category between Turner and public libraries. This could have been even higher since the Indianapolis Public Library

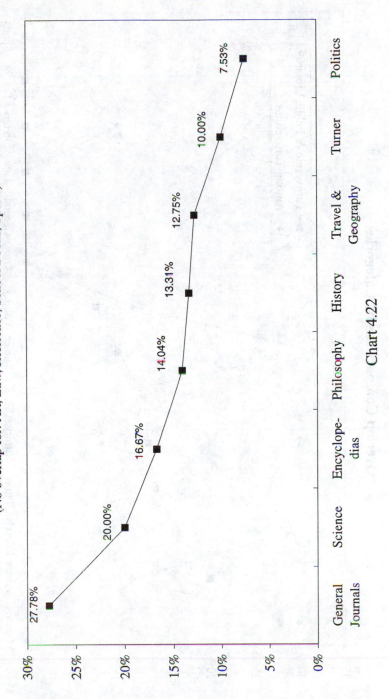

Overlap of Turnverein and Public Library German Holdings by Category

(No overlap for: Art, Law, Reference, School Books, Sports)

Chart 4.22

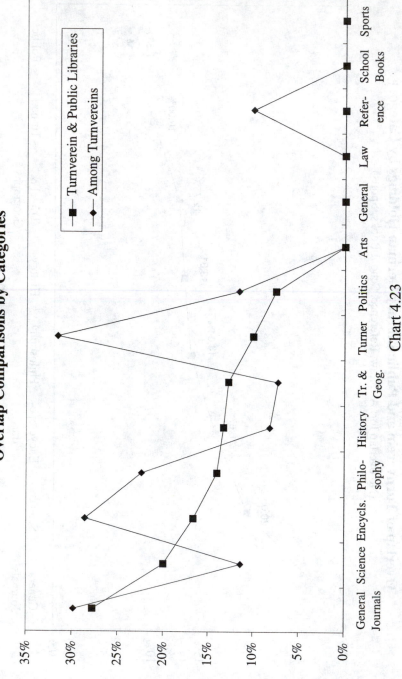

Overlap Comparisons by Categories

Chart 4.23

did not list any periodical titles in its German-language catalog, and it surely had some German-language subscriptions as evidenced by its current holdings of some German-language journal titles which date back to this period. Nevertheless, the relatively high percentage of overlap parallels a like overlap among the Turner libraries. Such titles included many of those already mentioned such as *Gartenlaube* (Leipzig), and *Illustrirte Zeitung*. Missing were subscriptions to more radical publications such as *Die Fackel* and *Der Arme Teufel*. But the St. Louis Public Library did carry a subscription to the German-American *Turnzeitung*, which was considered under the category of "Turner" below. Since the Indianapolis Public Library German-language catalog did not reflect the journal subscriptions, it is difficult to make any generalizations for this category. However, the high percentage overlap figure with even one library does suggest that this would hold true in a larger sampling. Ten of the fifteen titles that were owned by the public libraries were owned by more than one Turner library. Both the Turner and public libraries provided access to a great extent to a core of general informational German-language journals. Periodicals somewhat more controversial in nature appear not to have been held, but comparison with a greater sampling of public library holdings would be needed to confirm this.

"Science" titles overlapped by 20% of the holdings between Turner and public libraries. The St. Louis Public Library, with its strong science component, matched titles most frequently, but eight of the 33 matches were held in common by the public libraries. At times different works were held by the same author, but these were not counted as matches. This time the greater number of matches did not match the titles most held in common by the Turner libraries. Only seven of the 33 fell into this area, leaving the greatest percentage of matches with only one individual Turner library. The most held title by both the Turners and public libraries was Humboldt's *Kosmos*. The next most popular work held by four Turner and two public libraries was *Buch der Erfindungen, Gewerbe und Industrien*, or its successor *Das Neue Buch der Erfindungen* ... . Humboldt's *Ansichten der Natur* and Brehm's *Thierleben* were both held by three Turner libraries and the two public libraries. The Cincinnati Public Library also must have had a respected German-language science component since those were the titles thought important enough to provide access to for members of industry and university students during World War I when other areas of the German-language collection were inaccessible.[33]

All libraries had at least one general German-language encyclopedia. The most popular Turner library title, *Brockhaus' Conversations Lexikon* was held only by the St. Louis Public Library.

Although 14.04% of the titles in the "Philosophy" and 13.31% of the "Politics" categories overlapped between the Turner and public libraries, the more radical works were not generally held by the public libraries. The matches were more often for classical philosophy such as Plato and Cicero, although some more radical works were held by at least one public library, e.g., several works of Ferdinand Lassalle, including his *Arbeiterlesebuch*, Heinzen's *Teutsche Radikalismus in Amerika*, and Weitling's *Garantien der Harmonie und Freiheit*. Most of the more radical works that matched were titles held by the St. Louis Public Library, but the Indianapolis Public Library was the only public library maintaining works by Lassalle. Both public libraries owned works by Karl Marx, but none of the Turner libraries recorded any since the Turners generally considered themselves socialists, defending workers' rights, but not communists. Obviously the public libraries did not avoid radical topics, but the numbers of such works dominated these categories in the Turner collections. To find a wide variety of such works from authors like Louis Kossuth, August Bebel, and Samuel Ludvigh, the Turner would be more successful in his own library.

"History" and "Travel & Geography" overlapped more heavily by percentage of titles between public libraries and Turner libraries than among Turner libraries probably because of the larger holdings in these areas by the public libraries, increasing the probability that titles would match with one of the Turner libraries. "History" was the largest non-literature category by percentage of the Indianapolis Public Library German collection and the second highest for St. Louis. Curiously, the most held history title among Turner libraries, Gustav Struve's multi-volume *Weltgeschichte*, was not owned by either public library. Cazden relates that Struve's liberal and rationalistic views "had brought upon him the wrath of the religious press. Struve also claimed that priests in the confessional and elsewhere worked secretly against the distribution of his book."[34] Whether the latter was true or not, the title may have been considered too controversial for the public libraries. On the other hand, the St. Louis Public Library did own the work, *Deutsche Geschichte des XIX Jahrhunderts* by Treitschke, which was strongly anti-Turner in viewpoint and obviously was not owned by any Turner library. Of the 23 history titles owned by more than one Turner library, four were held by both public libraries and nine by at least one public library. In the category of "Travel & Geography" seven of the 11 titles held in common by more than one Turner library were also owned by a public library. Among the more popular titles by count were Wilhelm Heine's *Wanderbilder aus Central Amerika*, A. W. Grube's *Geographische Charakterbilder* . . . , and the German translated edition of Schlagintweit-Sakünlünski's *Reisen in Indien und Hochasien*.

Only two titles defined as "Turner" were held by a public library: the German-American *Turnzeitung*, and one book on gymnastics by Dr. Daniel Schreber. The St. Louis Public Library owned both of these. The Turner library in Indianapolis did have a strong collection of Turner or physical fitness literature which increased when it became the permanent site of the Normal College of the American Turners in 1907 although the total distribution of their titles cannot be reconstructed. Since the Turners were instrumental in promoting and achieving physical education as a requirement in the educational systems of both of these cities, one might have expected a greater number of titles in common. However, many of these titles may have been considered more instructional in nature and, hence, were not collected by the public libraries.

Chart 4.24 gives a graphic representation of the number of titles by non-literature categories held by the two largest Turner collections and the two public libraries. Chart 4.25 does the same for these groups in terms of percentage of collection for each category. Both public libraries had stronger collections in the "Fine Arts" than any of the Turner libraries. Music and theater were normally separate sections of the Turner organizations, and these sections may have kept some related publications separate as well. However, for the expressed interest in these cultural activities, little was reflected in the Turner libraries themselves other than primary works of drama in the literary component of the collections.

Comparison of Literary Works

Literature dominated all collections reviewed. A thorough comparison of the literary holdings needs further research, but several general observations can be made. A number of the German-American Forty-Eighters authors such as Karl Heinzen, Wilhelm Rothacker, Franz Joseph Egenter[35] were found only in the Turner library collections. Other German-American authors such as Heinrich Börnstein, Friedrich Hassaurek, Emil Klaupert, Theodor Griesinger, Georg Herwegh, and Reinhold Solger were either only represented or better represented in Turner libraries. The poetry of the German radical, Freiligrath, was readily available in most collections. Otto Ruppius was one "transatlantic author" prevalent in both Turner and public libraries. Ruppius was a moderate Forty-Eighter[36] who lived in the United States for almost twelve years and wrote many novels based on the experiences of German-Americans.[37] Osten reported in *The Milwaukee Turner* that the "Turners of Milwaukee apparently were deeply impressed with Otto Ruppius' work."[38]

Friedrich Gerstäcker, another author who wrote novels on life in America, appeared in almost every collection. Balduin Möllhausen also falls into this category and was held by three of five larger Turner libraries but none of the

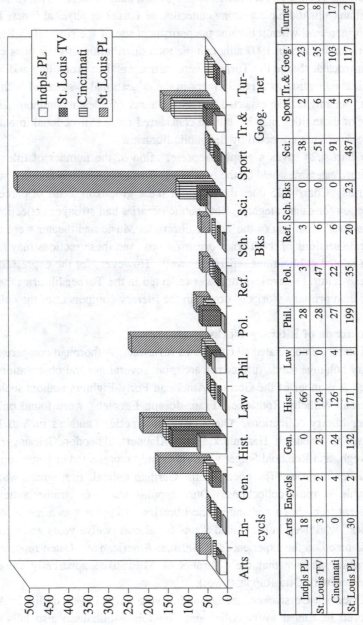

Comparison of Non-Literature Subject Categories

	Arts	Encycls	Gen.	Hist.	Law	Phil.	Pol.	Ref. Bks	Sch. Bks	Sci.	Sport	Tr.& Geog.	Turner
Indpls PL	18	1	0	66	1	28	3	3	0	38	2	23	0
St. Louis TV	3	2	23	124	0	28	47	6	0	51	6	35	8
Cincinnati	0	4	24	126	4	27	22	6	0	91	4	103	17
St. Louis PL	30	2	132	171	1	199	35	20	23	487	3	117	2

Chart 4.24

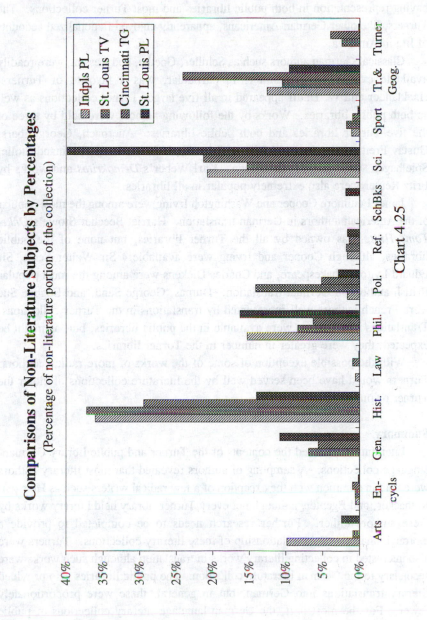

Comparisons of Non-Literature Subjects by Percentages
(Percentage of non-literature portion of the collection)

Chart 4.25

public libraries. These last two authors really did not qualify as German-Americans.[39] Charles Sealsfield (Karl Postl) was yet another author of such works as *Lebensbilder aus der westlichen Hemisphäre* who was highly popular, having representation in both public libraries and most Turner collections. The Turners, like other German-Americans, apparently enjoyed fictionalized accounts of life in America.

Classical German authors such as Schiller, Goethe, and Lessing were readily available everywhere. Schiller, in particular, was a favorite of Turners. Hackländer and W. Hauff appeared in all five larger Turner collections as well as both public libraries. Works by the following authors were held by three of the five Turner libraries and both public libraries: Auerbach, Georg Ebers, Gustav Freitag, Gutzkow, Mühlbach (Mundt), Heribert Rau, Ferdinand Stolle, Spielhagen, and Hans Wachenhusen. Karl Weber's *Demokritos* and works by Fritz Reuter were also extremely popular in all libraries.

James Fenimore Cooper and Washington Irving were among the most popular of the American authors in German translation. Harriet Beecher Stowe's *Onkel Toms Hütte* was owned by all the Turner libraries, but none of the public libraries, although Cooper and Irving were available. Sir Walter Scott, Sir Eduard Lytton, Shakespeare, and Charles Dickens were among the most popular British authors in German translation. Dumas, George Sand, and Eugene Sue were French authors well-represented by translations in the Turner collections. Translations into German were available in the public libraries, but, as might be expected, they were greater in number in the Turner libraries.

With the possible exception of some of the works of more radical authors, Turners would have been served well by the literature collections of either the Turner or public libraries.

Summary

Literature dominated the contents of the Turner and public library German-language collections. A sampling of authors revealed that most literary authors were held in common with the exception of a few radical writers such as Heinzen, Rothacker, and Egenter, although not every Turner library held literary works by these authors either. Further research needs to be completed to provide a thorough analysis of the relationship of these literary collections. Turners were also interested in collecting literary works in translation although such works were secondary to the German literature collection. The public libraries also provided literary translations into German, but in general, these were proportionately fewer. For the most part, the German-language literary collections of public libraries would have served the Turners well.

Although the percentages of holdings devoted to each subject category were very similar among the Turner libraries, a comparison of the non-literary titles held in common revealed that for specific titles the overall average of matching titles was approximately 31%. This indicates that while there is a common core of works, each collection has a uniqueness which is probably based on the specific interests and ready availability of other library resources of a given German-American community. Each Turner community would have to be studied in greater depth to understand better the dynamics for that location.

The comparison of the non-literary titles also indicated that many of the more radical writers would have been available to the Turners only through their own collections. This was also true for works dealing with gymnastics. It is clear that, as the radical political issues became less prominent in the Turner organizations, the public library German-language collections would have met the needs of Turner members, and the reasons for a separate library were greatly diminished.

NOTES

[1]Louisville Turngemeinde, Kentucky, List of Books from the Louisville Turnverein, 1990. This handwritten list was produced from the remaining volumes held at the Louisville Turners.

[2]The Aurora Turnverein (Chicago, IL) library remnants were discovered by the researcher at the Illinois Turners Camp in Elgin, IL. Along with the Aurora Turnverein were found volumes from the Turnverein Voran, and Turnverein Fortschritt, both from Chicago, IL, and some unidentified volumes. These volumes are now part of the Special Collections and Archives, IUPUI University Library, Indianapolis, IN.

[3]Max Kade German-American Document & Research Centre, University of Kansas, Lawrence, "Catalogue" (Lawrence, KS, 1976). Contains the remnants of the Milwaukee Turnverein library along with other holdings. The researcher had all Turnverein library holdings marked in a copy of the catalog from those volumes containing Milwaukee Turnverein book plates.

[4]Cincinnati Turngemeinde, *Katalog der Bibliothek der Turngemeinde in Cincinnati, April 1861* (Cincinnati, OH: Gedruckt bei Friedreich Lang, 1861), Cincinnati Historical Society, Cincinnati, OH; Cincinnati Turngemeinde, *Katalog der Bibliothek der Turn-Gemeinde in Cincinnati, O.* (Cincinnati, OH: Gedruckt bei Ad. Frey, 1866), Library of Congress, Washington, DC.

[5]St. Louis Turnverein, *Katalog der Bibliothek des St. Louis Turnvereins* (St. Louis, MO: Aug. Wiebusch Printing Co., 1895), Special Collections, Washington University Libraries, St. Louis, MO.

[6]Wilmington Turngemeinde, Catalog of Library Holdings, undated, Wilmington Turners Lodge Collection, Research Library, Balch Institute for Ethnic Studies, Philadelphia, PA.

[7]Katja Rampelmann, "Small Town Germans: The Germans of Lawrence, Kansas, from 1854 to 1918" (M.A. thesis, University of Kansas, Lawrence, 1993). Appendix III contains a listing of the Turnverein library.

[8]Ibid., 136.

[9]Don Heinrich Tolzmann, *German-American Literature* (Metuchen, N.J.: Scarecrow Press, 1977), ix-xi.

[10]Rampelmann, Appendix III.

[11]Ibid., 162.

[12]Harmut Keil, ed., *German Workers' Culture in the United States, 1850-1920* (Washington, D.C.: Smithsonian Institution Press, 1988), 50.

[13]Harmut Keil and John B. Jentz, eds., *German Workers in Chicago: A Documentary History of Working-Class Culture from 1850 to World War I* (Urbana, IL: University of Illinois Press, 1988), 167.

[14] Ibid., 250.

[15]Walter Osten, "The Milwaukee Turner Library," *Milwaukee Turner* 6, no.5 (May 1945): 1.

[16]Ibid.

[17]Milwaukee Turnverein, Paid invoices, Turner Society Collection, Milwaukee County Historical Society, Milwaukee, WI.

[18]Ed Schnetzky and W. Grisel, librarians, "Bericht der Bibliothekare des Zöglingsvereins des Turnvereins 'Milwaukee'," 13 January 1878, Turner Society Collection, Milwaukee County Historical Society, Milwaukee, WI; R. Schubert and A. Prier, librarians, "Halbjähriger Bericht der Bibliothekare des Zöglings Vereins," 4 August 1878, Turner Society Collection, Milwaukee County Historical Society, Milwaukee, WI.

[19]Deutsches Institut für Wissenschaft, Kunst und Gewerbe, *Catalog der Bibliothek* (St. Louis, MO: Gedruckt bei Klünder & Scholz, 1860), Special Collections, Washington University Libraries, St. Louis, MO.

[20]Ibid., 14.

[21]Ibid., 5.

[22]Robert E. Cazden, *A Social History of the German Book Trade in America to the Civil War*, Studies in German Literature, Linguistics, and Culture, vol. 1

(Columbia, SC: Camden House, 1984), 643.

[23]Ibid., 239.

[24]Indianapolis Public Library, *Finding List of the German and French Books in the Indianapolis Public Library: Authors and Titles* (Indianapolis: Carlon & Hollenbeck, Printers & Binders, 1885); Indianapolis Public Library, *Finding-List of the German and French Books in the Indianapolis Public Library: Authors and Titles* (Indianapolis: Issued by the Library, 1893).

[25]St. Louis Public Library, *Klassificirter Katalog ..., der Deutschen Werke in der Bibliothek der öffentlichen Schulen von St. Louis* (St. Louis, MO, 1880).

[26]American Turners, Minutes of the National Conventions, 1854–1872, tr. Henry W. Kumpf, undated, Typescript, Special Collections & Archives, IUPUI University Library, Indianapolis, IN, 405.

[27]Ibid.

[28]Ibid., 451, 547.

[29]See Cazden, *A Social History*, 502–512, for a discussion of the *Freie Gemeinde* and religious reform as related to publications.

[30]Ibid., 318.

[31]Ibid.

[32]American Turners, Minutes, 1866, 406–07.

[33]Guido A. Doebbert, *The Disintegration of an Immigrant Community: The Cincinnati Germans, 1870–1920* (New York: Arno, 1988), 394.

[34]Cazden, *A Social History*, 397–8.

[35]Ibid., 382–386.

[36]Ibid., 388.

[37]Ibid., 387.

[38]Walter Osten, "Turner Library Favors Early American History," *The Milwaukee Turner* 6, no. 7 (July 1945): 4.

[39]Cazden, *A Social History*, 386.

V

USE

One of the most critical factors in understanding the role of a library in an organization is the use of the collection. However, in this study, information about use of the collections is one of the most elusive factors. In the geographical area under close scrutiny here, the only references found to use are tangential ones in minutes or reports referring to the need to expand library quarters (Aurora Turnverein, Chicago) and complaints about non-return of titles (New Ulm, Minnesota). Turner records indicate that logs of borrowers and titles were kept for most organizations which were studied. Unfortunately, these record books could not be located.

The discovery of a borrowers' record book for the Wilmington Turngemeinde (Deleware)[1] prompted the inclusion of this organization for the usage aspect, though it does not fall in the specific geographic area of the primary study. With the borrowers' record book (1906–1932) was also found a catalog of the collection (undated)[2] and the actual remnants of the library. These materials and several other primary resources are now being housed at the Balch Institute for Ethnic Studies, Philadelphia, Pennsylvania. These materials provide a unique opportunity to compare the contents of a discrete collection with its recorded use.

The physical description of the borrowers' record book is useful in understanding the nature of the data kept and its effect on any analysis. The book is stamped with the ownership of the Wilmington Turngemeinde. In addition, the embossed stamp appears: H. WIDDEKIND. TEACHER OF PHYSICAL CULTURE. In script on the same page is the word "Bibliothek." This might be an indication that the physical education instructor was responsible for the preservation of these records even if he did not actually record the information. The "Constitution and Bylaws" from 1885[3] and 1895[4] indicate that there was a Library Committee and an office of Librarian. The latter conforms to those present in many other Turner organizations, such as New Ulm and Cincinnati, in which the librarian held responsibility for such loans.

In the front of the book is a roughly alphabetical index of names referring to the pages on which can be found the loan record for the individual named. This index of names is not complete although differences in handwriting indicate that attempts to update the index were made by more than one record keeper. Differences in handwriting style and recording style within the borrowers' entries also reflect multiple record keepers. A chronological loan record was entered under each borrower's name. Entries are recorded either by the class number or the title's sequential number and occasionally only by title. For example, E34 might also have been recorded as E114 since E34 was also listed as No. 114 sequentially. This is mentioned because of the confusion sometimes created in analyzing the entries. There were a few "sequential" numbers which occurred in more than one instance although it appears that unique sequential numbers were attempted. There is a B2, No. 53 but there was also a C53, No. 53. Fortunately, an author or part of a title was sometimes supplied to assist in identifying items checked out when ambiguity of numbers was present. The "confusion" in sequential numbers occurs most frequently when items were added to the end of a classification sequence in the handwritten catalog.[5] There were also numbers recorded as loans which do not have entries in the book catalog, e.g., E64 and E192, even though numbers around them did exist in the catalog. Since these loans occurred in late entries within the loan records, one must assume they correspond to later, unrecorded acquisitions. A few very late loan entries also have fragments of titles or names which do not correspond to catalog entries or library remains, nor do they contain enough information to identify them. These five items are noted as unidentified in the analysis since neither their subjects nor their languages can be discerned with any certainty.

There are 68 borrowers' names listed with entries. Of these, two names are repeated on later pages with more recent records. For this study these two names are treated as the same person since this currently cannot be otherwise verified and does little to distort the analysis.

Five borrowers were females, two of which appear to have male relatives who also signed out materials. The women signed out books an average of two times, borrowing an average of 2.3 volumes per loan. The men charged materials an average of 3.13 times per person with an average of 2 volumes per loan. Of course, it is impossible to know from these records if the male members signed out materials for themselves only or for family members also. Most borrowers in both groups signed out materials only once or twice, 68.3% of the time for men and 80% of the time for women. Thus, relatively few people account for multiple loans. The person having the highest number of charges had 25 loans for a total of 71 volumes over a two-year period. Those borrowers responsible for the higher number of charges also tended to take two or more volumes at a time and over a continuous chronological period, demonstrating a sustained interest in the use of the collection.

What subjects did these borrowers actually read from the collection? How did what they read compare to the overall content of the library? And how did such use and content compare to the stated mission of the library? Collection content is analyzed elsewhere in this study. Given the relative similarity of subjects across geographical regions, the use of this particular collection takes on added significance. As already cautioned, each German-American community had unique characteristics, but the Turners tried to maintain similar goals for their organizations nationwide and some cautious extrapolations might be made, bolstered by additional collaborating evidence.

The mission of this library must first be identified. The "Freibrief der Wilmington Turngemeinde (1885)," stating the incorporation and purpose of this organization is given in German in the 1888 printing of its constitution[6] and in English in the 1895 version.[7] The Wilmington Turngemeinde was founded 10 November 1859, and incorporated 19 February 1885. The library is listed prominently in the stated purpose of the organization in this 1885 statement. The quotation below is taken from the English version:

> SECTION 2. The object of the said corporation shall be the intellectual and physical improvement of the members by forming and keeping up a library, by establishing schools and by furnishing instruction in gymnastic exercises.[8]

Among the *Rechte und Pflichten der Vorstandsmitglieder* is the advancement of the library,[9] and the librarian is listed as one of the major officers.[10] Both elements support the value of the library function within the organization. As discussed under organizational structure, the above evidence suggests that the library was considered an important component of this Turngemeinde's mission.

As with other Turnvereins, the 1889 *Constitution und Nebengesetze* gave no direct collection development mandate, although the librarian had to give a status report each six months and present his successor with a thorough report. The 1895 *Platform, Constitution und Nebengesetze* directions to the Library Committee referred only to permission for the Committee to buy materials "von Zeit zu Zeit, oder wenn sich günstige Gelegenheit bieten sollte" (from time to time or when a propitious occasion should arise)[11] as long as a set yearly amount is not overreached. The types of materials to be purchased are not detailed here. One must really go back to the purpose of the specific organization and the national federation, then called Nordamerikanischer Turnerbund, to ascertain the library's general purpose. This is discussed more fully under the chapter on content of collections.

It is known that the platform changed somewhat over time for both the local and national bodies. Therefore, the purpose stated in the same local *Constitution und Nebengesetze* will be used to measure purpose and to avoid crossing time periods between instructions to the librarians and library committees and the purposes stated. The 1895 booklet features the national platform of the Nordamerikanischer Turnerbund (North American Turnerbund) prominently as the first item.[12] The passage most pertinent to this discussion stressed the propagation of education and the support of morality as the only means of thorough reform in social, political, and religious areas:

> Wir erkennen in der Verbreitung von Bildung und in der Pflege von Sittlichkeit die einzigen Mittel zur gründlichen Reform auf socialem, politischem und religiösem Gebiete.
>
> Wir befürworten und erstreben die Entwicklung des Volksstaats auf wahrhaft humaner und volksthümlicher Basis. Jeder Versuch zur Beschränkung der Gewissensfreiheit, so wie alle Rechtsverkürzungen, welche der Vervollkommnung und dem Ausbau unserer freiheitlichen Institutionen widerstreben, werden deshalb von uns auf das Entschiedenste bekämpft.[13]

Likewise, the previously quoted passage from Wilmington spoke in general terms of improving the intellectual development of its members in order to help them become informed, conscientious citizens.[14] However, as described in the chapter on content, when comparing size of subject content, the library collections do not reflect a strong predilection to political theses. Rather, the vast majority of materials were in the literary realm, with that of German literature predominating.

Does usage follow the same pattern as the actual subject distribution? Does the subject distribution follow that of the broadly stated purpose? The general subject categories referred to here for the Wilmington Turngemeinde correspond with those stated under content. Particular difficulty was encountered in trying to count the circulation of general journal titles since it was frequently unclear how many volumes or issues were loaned per title. Therefore, each journal loan was counted as one volume of a title to maintain some kind of consistency in data analyses. This will cause a slight error on the lower side in the number of items circulated. This seemed preferable to the researcher, rather than overestimating journal volumes circulated when multiple issues cited may actually have been bound together as one volume if this collection followed the binding practices of other Turner libraries examined.

The categories of "General" and "Journals" are combined in this analysis since the journals included tended to be multi-disciplinary in nature.

The table below shows that the largest category, literature, was also the one that circulated most. One hundred and two of 139 literary volumes or 73.38% were loaned out. According to percentages of those volumes actually borrowed, only the history category outweighed this amount (80.77%) although the number of literary works far outnumbered history in volumes owned by the library. Only the literary category had more multiple charges than any other group (see Table 5.1; additional graphic representations in Charts 5.1-5.2). Of those items charged more than four times, literature had 45 while the only competing category, history, had one.

	Total Volumes	Number Charged At Least Once	% Charged
History	26	21	80.77%
Literature	139	102	73.38%
Politics	12	8	66.67%
General	21	13	61.9 %
Philosophy	2	1	50.0 %
Science	19	7	36.84%
Travel & Geography	6	1	16.67%
Reference	22	0	00.0 %
Sports	2	0	00.0 %
Turner	2	0	00.0 %
Unknown	5	5	100.0 %
TOTAL:	256	158	62.72%

(See also Chart 5.3)

It might be assumed that the reference volumes were not allowed to circulate since this is common practice in most libraries. If reference volumes are excluded as non-circulating items, then 67.52% of the volumes would have been circulated at least once in a period of 26 years. The two Turner books are histories of the American Turners, one in English and one in German. These may have been considered reference in nature or ones which most members had already purchased for themselves.

When actual frequency of charges are examined, the predominance of literary charges is quite evident:

WILMINGTON TURNGEMEINDE
Library Borrowers' Record Book

CHARGES OF VOLUMES BY SUBJECT:

IN CATALOG:

	Gen.	Hist.	Lit.	Phil.	Pol.	Ref.	Sci.	Sports	Tr&G	Turner	SUM:	% of Charges In Cat.
No Charges:	8	5	37	1	4	22	12	2	5	2	98	45.37%
1 Charge:	1	4	29	1	5	0	3	0	0	0	43	19.91%
2 Charges:	3	7	14	0	2	0	1	0	1	0	28	12.96%
3 Charges:	1	3	1	0	1	0	0	0	0	0	6	2.78%
4 Charges:	0	1	4	0	0	0	2	0	0	0	7	3.24%
5 Charges:	0	0	9	0	0	0	0	0	0	0	9	4.17%
6 Charges:	0	1	9	0	0	0	0	0	0	0	10	4.63%
7 Charges:	0	0	9	0	0	0	0	0	0	0	9	4.17%
8 Charges:	0	0	6	0	0	0	0	0	0	0	6	2.78%
	13	21	118	2	12	22	18	2	6	2	216	
% by Category	6.02%	9.72%	54.63%	0.93%	5.56%	10.19%	8.33%	0.93%	2.78%	0.93%		

NOT IN CATALOG:

	Gen.	Hist.	Lit.	Phil.	Pol.	Ref.	Sci.	Sports	Tr&G	Unknown	SUM:	% of Charges
1 Charge:	7	5	20	0	0	0	0	0	0	5	37	92.50%
2 Charges:	0	0	1	0	0	0	0	0	0	0	1	2.50%
3 Charges:	0	0	0	0	0	0	1	0	0	0	1	2.50%
4 Charges:	1	0	0	0	0	0	0	0	0	0	1	2.50%
	8	5	21	0	0	0	1	0	0	5	40	
% by Category	20.00%	12.50%	52.50%	0.00%	0.00%	0.00%	2.50%	0.00%	0.00%	12.50%		

Table 5.1

WILMINGTON TURNGEMEINDE
Library Borrowers' Record Book

CHARGES OF VOLUMES BY SUBJECT:

COMBINED CHARGES:

	Gen.	Hist.	Lit.	Phil.	Pol.	Ref.	Sci.	Sports	Tr&G	Turner	Unknown	SUM:	% of Total Vols.	% of Charged Items Only
No Charges:	8	5	37	1	4	22	12	2	5	2	0	98	38.28%	
1 Charge:	8	9	49	1	5	0	3	0	0	0	5	80	31.25%	50.63%
2 Charges:	3	7	15	0	2	0	1	0	1	0	0	29	11.33%	18.35%
3 Charges:	1	3	1	0	1	0	1	0	0	0	0	7	2.73%	4.43%
4 Charges:	1	1	4	0	0	0	2	0	0	0	0	8	3.13%	5.06%
5 Charges:	0	0	9	0	0	0	0	0	0	0	0	9	3.52%	5.70%
6 Charges	0	1	9	0	0	0	0	0	0	0	0	10	3.91%	6.33%
7 Charges:	0	0	9	0	0	0	0	0	0	0	0	9	3.52%	5.70%
8 Charges:	0	0	6	0	0	0	0	0	0	0	0	6	2.34%	3.80%
Total Vols.	21	26	139	2	12	22	19	2	6	2	5	256		
Vols. Charged	13	21	102	1	8	0	7	0	1	0	5	158		
% Charged	8.23%	13.29%	64.56%	0.63%	5.06%	0.00%	4.43%	0.00%	0.63%	0.00%	3.16%	% of Total Vols.		

Table 5.1 (cont.)

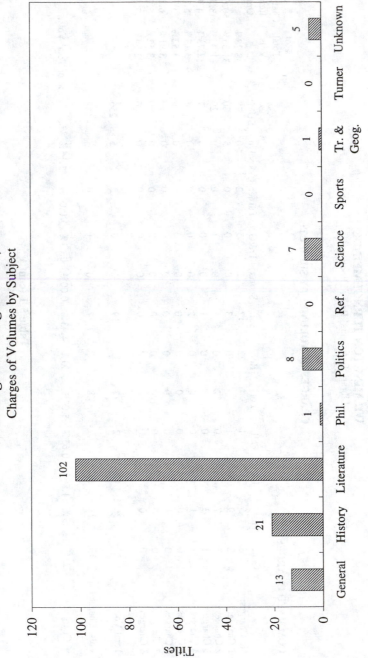

Wilmington Turngemeinde, DE
Charges of Volumes by Subject

Chart 5.1

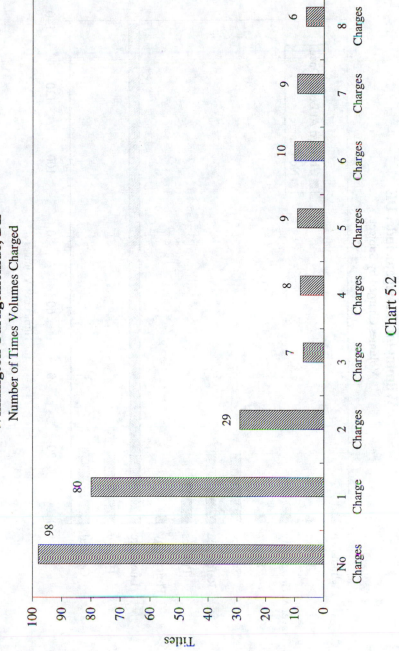

Wilmington Turngemeinde, DE
Number of Times Volumes Charged

Chart 5.2

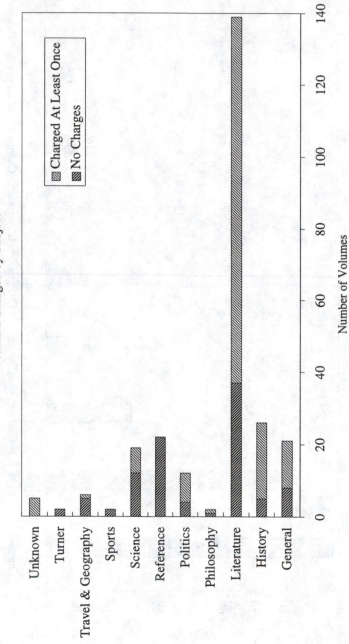

Wilmington Turngemeinde, DE
Volumes Charged by Subject

Chart 5.3

	Charges	% of Total Charges
Literature	308	75.68%
History	42	10.32%
General	21	5.16%
Science	16	3.93%
Politics	12	2.95%
Unknown	5	1.23%
Travel & Geography	2	0.50%
Philosophy	1	0.25%
Reference	0	0.00%
Sports	0	0.00%
Turner	0	0.00%
TOTAL:	407	100.02% (Caused by rounding off)

It is clear that "Literature" was the category most charged by the Wilmington Turngemeinde members. This paralleled the experience of most contemporary public libraries.[15] However, these usage patterns do not seem to support the stated major purposes of the organization in promoting an informed citizenry through its library unless one takes the stance that a well-read person, regardless of the subject matter, is a well-educated, informed person. Usage does indicate that the books owned were in large proportion well-used, in that 61.72% (67.52% excluding reference volumes) of the collection was signed out at least once.

One category not included in this breakdown of subjects is newspapers. None are listed in the Wilmington Turngemeinde catalog although several other Turnvereins (Cincinnati, New Ulm) indicated that they at least had subscriptions to local newspapers available for their members. It is very probable that newspaper subscriptions were also held at Wilmington but were not listed in the catalog since they were probably not retained for any length of time. Newspapers would have been another mechanism to keep members informed on current events.

Another category that possibly contributed to the overall knowledge of members was that of "General." The "General" category did include general journals such as *Deutsche Illustrirte Zeitung*, which contained articles about worldwide events. However, the journal holdings listed in the catalog were for only a few years in the 1870s and 1880s, indicating that these may have been gifts and not ongoing subscriptions. The recorded circulation of journals not listed in the catalog were for later years, indicating a possible subscription or continuous gift. When the general age of the journal issues is compared to the time of the borrowing log, it is no wonder that few of these items were checked out. Those titles which were checked out corresponded to those found in many other Turnverein collections: *Die Gartenlaube*, *Rundschau zweier Welten*, *Vom Fels zum Meer*, *German-American Annals*. Only two titles held were in English, *German-American Annals* (1904–05) and one 1881 uncirculated volume of *Scientific American*, listed as "*Scientific of Amerika*." Over half, 61.9%, of the "General" volumes were charged out, indicating an interest in the later volumes of general topic serials.

A further break-down of charges reveals some interesting additional information about the overall use and characteristics of this collection. The division of the collection by language is as follows:

	Volumes	Percentage	Translations	% of Language
English	42	16.41%	4	9.50%
German	209	81.64%	16*	7.66%
Unknown	5	1.95%		
TOTAL:	256	100.00%	20	17.16%

(*11 of the 209 volumes in German could not be identified as to translation status.)

Obviously, the largest portion of the collection was in German. The only other language represented in the Wilmington Turngemeinde library was English. These are also the primary languages of other Turnverein libraries, but other libraries also contained some works in other languages. Very few of the German-language items in the Wilmington collection were translations from other languages. Of those which were translations ten out of sixteen were never signed out. Two of those not circulated were "Reference" titles translated from Swedish. A further breakdown of these translations by subject is given below:

Subject	Volumes	Charged Volumes	Total Charges
American History	5	2	4

Subject	Volumes	Charged Volumes	Total Charges
Reference	2	0	0
French Literature	2	1	5
Science	2	0	0
Politics	2	2	4
General Literature	1	0	0
General History	1	1	1
Travel & Geography	1	0	0

One French novel accounted for the most charges with "American History" and "Politics" reflecting the next highest use of translations. The two volumes of American history most used were one on Abraham Lincoln by Joseph Barrett and one on the Johnstown flood. The latter was also held in the original English. The English version was signed out twice as well. The two in the category of "Politics" were: 1) a bilingual edition of E. B. Washburne's *America's Aid to Germany, 1870–71* (1905), with three charges, and 2) a book on parliamentary practice with one charge. The researcher put Washburne's book in the "Politics" category instead of "History" since it dealt with relations between the United States and Germany. The title on parliamentary practice might also be categorized as "Reference," but since it was the only one of its kind that was actually loaned, the researcher designated it under "Politics" with the assumption the borrowers were trying to understand political organizational procedures.

Four volumes in English were translations. Only two of the four were from the German and both were translations of German literature collections. Of these two titles, only one was loaned and that only once. One translation was a version of *The Arabian Nights*, which was never charged out, and the other was an English translation of Louis Du Couret's *Life in the Desert, Asia and Africa* (1860).

Subject	Volumes	Charged Volumes	Total Charges
German Literature	2	1	1
General Literature	1	0	0
Travel & Geography	1	1	2

Clearly, translations did not represent a significant portion of the library collection. Literature was primarily collected and read in the original version whether that was German or English. French literature was the only exception with two volumes translated into German and with only one of the two being charged out, but there were only two volumes of French literature in this collection.

German literature far outweighed any other category of literature at 113 volumes or 81.3%. Not only was this the largest portion of the literature collection, but it was also the most used portion. German literature accounted for all multiple charges of volumes from four to eight charges except for six. Of the total of 407 charges, 276 or 67.8% of all charges were German literature. For this analysis, any literature published in German which was not translated was considered German literature. A few of these titles are known to have been by German-American authors publishing in German.

Of the German literature titles, those classified as "Classics" in the Wilmington Turngemeinde catalog were the least signed out by borrowers. Fifty-four volumes of German literature were in this grouping. One volume of Horace was also classified here. Twenty-five volumes (46.3%) were never borrowed, whereas only five volumes in other German literature classifications were never loaned. Large sets of Schiller, Goethe, Heine, and Kleist comprised most of the "Classic" titles. All volumes of Heine were read as well as some volumes of Goethe and Schiller, but no volumes of Kleist were signed out. The "Classics" group accounted for 48 charges of the 276, or 17.4%, recorded for German literature. Only two "Classics" volumes were signed out more than two times. One of these was a volume of Schiller (four charges) and the other a volume of Gerstäcker's works, *Blau Wasser* (seven charges). It might well be expected that any German-American library of worth would contain these major classics. At the same time, it would be expected that anyone with a private library would also own some edition of these major classics. This could account for less use of these items from the library. It is known from the remnants of some private German-American libraries examined in Indianapolis that such works would have been represented in private collections.

The most used volumes of German literature primarily reflected titles listed under the classification of "*Romane & Novellen*" and within that classification under the general heading: "*Original Beiträge: verschiedener Schriftsteller und Gelehrten, Jahrgang ____.*" Titles of individual volumes are listed by each year. Each of these volumes has a Wilmington Turngemeinde Library classification number. Some titles continued from one volume to the next. Authors were not given, and the researcher was not able to locate the individual titles in the national bibliographic utility, OCLC. The years given were 1879, 1880, and 1888. Each year contained twelve volumes. These volumes, with the exception of seven from other local classifications, accounted for all multiple charges over three. These may have been volumes in the series, *Bibliothek der Unterhaltung und des Wissens*, since the years and volumes given match most closely to this title discovered in the remnants of the Wilmington Turngemeinde library. Remnants of this title were nine volumes for 1879, ten volumes for 1880, nine volumes for 1888, and four volumes for 1891. This series was also found in other Turnverein collections. Each volume contained one or more stories or essays. Its usage in this collection and its appearance in multiple volumes in other Turnverein collections indicate that this was a very popular title for German-American Turnverein readers.

English literature, either British or American, was the next highest literature type held with twelve volumes or 8.6% of all literature volumes. Eight of these twelve volumes (66.67%) were signed out at least once. However, only one title, Ned Buntline's *Buffalo Bill*, was signed out more than once. This particular title must have been popular since it was charged five times. (Only 34 volumes were charged five times or more.) General or world literature comprised only two volumes, a volume of Horace and a version of *The Arabian Nights*, neither which was loaned.

A closer examination of the "History" volumes shows that American history was the predominant topic for collecting and use within this category. Nineteen of the 26 volumes (73.1%) fell in the category of American history. Unlike the literature area, the predominant language in this category was German regardless of subject. Thus, American history had twelve of its nineteen volumes in German with five being translations and another five volumes, all of one title, unclear as to their original language. Only four of the American history titles were never signed out. The complete history break down is as follows:

	Language	Volumes	Total Charges
General History	German	2	1
American History	German	12	12
	English	7	19
French History	German	1	1
German History	German	4	9

The chart above shows that even though there were fewer titles in English, they were the titles most circulated. The most popular history title with six loans for the first volume of the three-volume set was Gustavus Myers' *History of the Great American Fortunes*. The other two volumes of the set were signed out four and two times respectively. This title was published about 1910 and conceivably could have been more popular because of its later publication date.

Those American history volumes not signed out comprised three titles. One was a two-volume set on the American Civil War which was translated from English and published in German also simultaneously with the English versions. Both language versions were published in the 1860s. The other two works were Ridpath's work on the life of James Garfield (German translation) and a history of Swiss colonies in the United States by Steinbach (in German).

Three of the four German history volumes are represented by one title, Theodor Ebner's *Illustrierte Geschichte Deutschlands*. The fourth volume dealt with war between Germany and France. All of these volumes circulated at least twice. The one French history volume dealt with the French Revolution.

The circulation of history volumes demonstrates that the Turnverein readers were more interested in their adopted homeland and more frequently read about that topic in English even though the subject was better represented by German-language volumes.

In the subject category of science, ten out of the nineteen volumes of Brehm's *Thierleben* were circulated. Although only half of these volumes had been signed out, those charges accounted for all but four of the sixteen total charges for science. The other four charges were for Berge's *Naturgeschichte* (one charge) and a title on medical practices (three charges). Other subjects represented, but never circulated, were astronomy, evolution, mathematics, and information about scientists.

Although the political category represented a small segment of the total library collection (twelve out of 256 volumes, or 4.69%), the volumes were well-used. At 66.67%, this was the third highest category as regards the percentage of volumes circulated, following that of history and literature. The types of books held and circulated were similar to those in other Turnverein libraries. The most loaned title was a translation into German about America's help to Germany in 1870–71. Karl Heinzen, one of the more prolific and well-respected German-American Forty-Eighters, was represented by four works in this collection, and all but one had been signed out. A volume by Bebel (*Die Frau und Sozialismus*), one by Engels (*Der Ursprung der Familie, des Privateigenthums und des Staats*), one on temperance, and one about Free Thinkers helped complete the liberal direction of this category. In this respect, the collection was true to the liberal causes and thinking supported by the German-American Turners. And while the circulation may not have been as high as either history or literature, their usage was proportionally significant.

Did the collection fulfill its goal to challenge its members intellectually and make them informed, critical-thinking citizens? The above evidence would indicate that similar to public library collections of the period, the literature or fiction collections were the most prominent and most signed out in terms of numbers. When proportionate usage within a category is examined, the history and the political categories compete strongly with literature. The area of general information was also proportionately well-utilized for the number of volumes held. If one assumes that a well-read and well-cultured person contributes to an informed citizenry, then this goal was met. However, the content and usage does seem to correspond more to that of what would be expected in a public library with the significant exception of the well-used, liberal political holdings. Harmut Keil has confirmed the use of "pulp and schmaltz fiction—sentimental novels ... adventure, cloak-and-dagger novels from Ganghofer to Gerstäcker ..." even by such socialist publications as the *Fackel*.[16] The working-man and Turner needed some break from the tedium of the day.

The fact that about two-thirds of the collection was used at some time during this borrowing period supports the value of this collection to its users. The availability of German literature, general topics, and liberal political information in German was well-received by the readers. American history and English literature were preferred in English. Reviewing when these materials were signed out also established important information on usage patterns. Chart 5.4 shows the distribution of charges by year to the degree that the year could be identified. Unfortunately a large number of circulation records did not give the year. Most, but not all, of the later entries were identified by year. Even if one assigned all unknown years to the pre-1913 period, the year with which dates seem to become more regularly recorded, a little over half of the items would have been signed out from 1914 onward. The chart shows, however, that usage started to decline from 1916 onward with the exception of 1925. This decline in usage would parallel the decline in new German immigrants to the United States and the probable increased presence of second generation, English-speaking members.

The section on content of collections demonstrated the similarity of subject distribution across geographical regions. It would seem that some similarities in usage could also be expected based on these patterns. Support for this proposition was given by the librarian, Poole, in *Public Libraries in the United States* in 1876: "'Statistics show that the taste for reading in one community is the same

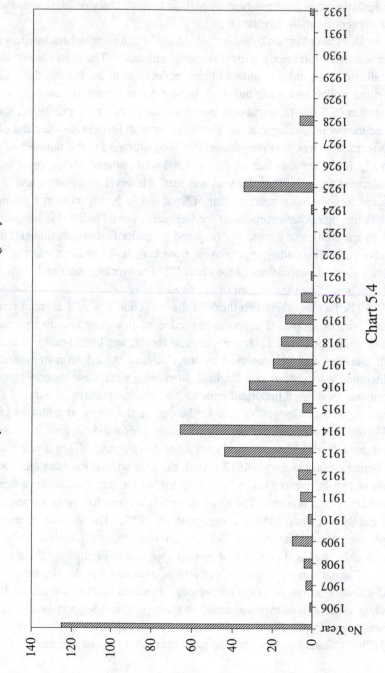

Wilmington Turngemeinde, DE

Library Borrowers' Record Book - Charges by Year

Chart 5.4

as that of every other community in similar social conditions.'"[17] Bergquist has pointed out that:

> . . . glimpses of other German urban communities make the point that experiences could vary considerably, depending on what kinds of Germans came to a particular place, when they came, the kinds of opportunities they sought and found, and the kinds of social and economic environments they entered.[18]

Turnvereins were no exceptions to these conditions, varying somewhat in activities and degree of adherence to national Turner platforms depending on urban or rural environments, societal status, economic levels of members, and date of establishment. However, Turnvereins, similar to other ethnic social organizations, were community centers for German immigrant groups, providing mutual support and activities. Thus the Turner libraries under scrutiny here could be expected to have very similar proportional subject content, even when the library sizes differed. The statements from minutes or reports and secondary sources are among the only usage clues discovered for the other organizations under the primary study. The sizes of these collections over time and the availability of other library collections with German-language materials provide additional clues to usage.

In the examples below, it is impossible to give complete coverage of all the factors that might affect the Turnvereins' library development and usage since any of the major cities covered warrant complete studies in themselves. For example, 36 Turnvereins were reported to the national Turners during the period from 1866 to 1920 in Chicago alone. Also, there were often other Turnvereins that did not belong to the national groups. Thus, information provided had to rely on those organizations for which the researcher was able to locate collections, minutes, or other primary materials. Nevertheless, predictive patterns developed. Growth in collections, indicating interest and usage, seem to depend on such factors as: 1) date of establishment, 2) existence and availability of other German-language library collections, and 3) the community in which the Turnverein existed.

Aurora Turnverein, Chicago, Illinois

No minutes from the Aurora Turnverein (Chicago, Illinois) were located by the researcher. The only evidence found of library use there was in statements quoted by Harmut Keil in his work, *German Workers in Chicago*, from an article about the Aurora Turnverein published in *Der Westen: Frauen-Zeitung* on 15 and 22 November 1896. In this historical overview of the Aurora Turnverein the library was mentioned several times. One such statement directly referred to usage:

> Because of the large run on the library, the Verein determined, on April 21, 1884, to rent and furnish two rooms to be used as library and reading rooms.[19]

Mention was also made of the establishment of another library for those "pupils" who were younger:

> A library for Turn pupils was founded on September 10; suitable books and other reading material were acquired, and this not only attracted young people, but also helped in furthering the German language.[20]

Separate libraries for younger Turner members were not uncommon. Such libraries were also established in Cincinnati and Milwaukee.

In addition, when the article quoted by Keil discussed the popularity of "informal educational get-togethers and regularly scheduled evening debates," reference was made to the preparation of members "who generally acquainted themselves with books from the library pertaining to the topics under discussion so as to be able to join in the debates."[21]

Other Turner libraries in Chicago varied in size from zero to 2,100 volumes as reported in the national statistics from 1866 to 1920. The Aurora Turnverein and the Chicago Turngemeinde had the largest collections, each of which numbered at least 2,000 volumes at one point in time. Harmut Keil has pointed out the importance of these Turnvereins within the Chicago community groups, however this researcher was unable to ascertain with certainty why either group developed and used its own library collection. The information found for other communities described below and predictive indicators found through statistical analysis, treated later, give the reader some indication of what these factors might have been. Of the 36 Chicago Turnvereins listed in the national Turner statistics, 28 (77.8%) did have libraries. However, only 25% had collections of 500 volumes and over. Other categories were: 200 to 499 volumes, 5 (13.9%); 100 to 299 volumes, 4 (11.1%); 10 to 99 volumes, 10 (27.8%); no volumes reported, 8 (22.2%). Thus, the majority of Turner organizations followed the national recommendation to establish libraries, but only a fourth of them built major collections which might indicate higher importance and usage to their respective local groups.

Indianapolis, Indiana

As described earlier, the library of the Indianapolis Turnverein was also that of the Normal College of the North American Gymnastic Union from 1907 until 1941 when its merger with Indiana University deeded over this material to the University. However, since the classes were still held at the Athenaeum, home of the Indianapolis Turners, until 1970, this library remained available to members. No specific information was found on the early usage of the collection, but purchases, particularly after the permanent establishment in 1907 of the Normal College in Indianapolis, remained steady, indicating an actively used collection. Even as late as the 1940s much of this collection was still in the German-language. The statistical information reported to the national headquarters of the American Turners indicated that the collection grew from 150 volumes in 1851 to 563 volumes in 1920. However, the first record of the size of the Normal College Library which appeared in the Indiana University Libraries' annual reports in 1944/45 was 2,025 volumes. Either there had been a major increase during these twenty years or the Indianapolis Turnverein reported its holdings separate from the Normal College holdings. It is known from the 1898 building plans for the Athenaeum that provision was made for a library and reading room. This, of course, happened before the Normal College became a permanent occupant of Das Deutsche Haus (after 1918, The Athenaeum). In 1970 when the Normal College, renamed the IUPUI School of Physical Education, moved to a new, leased location on 64th Street, many of the predominantly German-language titles in the library were offered to the faculty members and the rest were sent to the Bloomington campus of Indiana University.[22]

The identified remnants of the Indianapolis Turnverein library were primarily those related to physical education and reflected the mission of the Normal College. At the time of the permanent establishment of the Normal College in Indianapolis there would have been no need for it to expend funds on general literature since the Indianapolis Public Library,[23] established in 1873, had an extensive German-language collection. Separate catalogs of the German- and French-language materials in the Indianapolis Public Library were published in 1885 and 1893. These catalogs and the nature of these collections were discussed under the earlier chapter on contents. A distinctively larger portion of these catalogs were for German-language holdings than of French-language books. Thus, German-language materials were easily obtainable within close geographical proximity and were well used by the German community. An 1873–74 report by the Indianapolis Public Library librarian Charles Evans, recorded that the German and French collections were the most used category

among its holdings (5.0% of the year's charges) after that of fiction at 77.8%.[24]
This was at a time before printed catalogs of the Indianapolis Public Library
holdings were available to the public and when the stacks were not yet open for
browsing. This would indicate that German-speaking readers actively pursued the
use of this collection. Consequently it would not have been necessary for the
Indianapolis Turnverein to provide the kind of general reading materials often
found in other Turnverein collections lacking such ready access nearby.

The South Side Turnverein in Indianapolis never emphasized its library.
Little was recorded in its minutes regarding the library collection even though the
South Side Turners had its own Turner Hall and a sizeable membership. Its later
establishment in 1893, the local availability of a good public library collection,
and the later presence of the Normal College specialized collection would easily
have been contributing factors to this lack of emphasis on a proprietary library
resource. It did establish a small library, however, that grew from 30 volumes
in 1895 to 118 volumes in 1920 according to its periodic reports to the national
organization.

New Ulm, Minneapolis and St. Paul, Minnesota

Only fragments of information about library usage at the New Ulm
(Minnesota) Turners organization can be gleaned from its minutes. On the 6th
of March 1875 it decided at a closed session that a list of all missing books would
be posted at every meeting until the books were returned. This list included the
library numbers and titles of the books and the names of the borrowers, if known.
Some are crossed off in the minutes, as perhaps members returned the books
later. The request for the return of borrowed books seemed to be a recurring
theme in the minutes, for example, mentioned again in the 4 March 1876 and 11
October 1884 minutes.

On 20 March 1875 it was resolved that the students of the public schools
could visit the Turner "school library" on one evening per week. Indeed,
relations between the more "radical" Turners and the general community of New
Ulm seemed to be quite amicable for some time as is shown in a citation in
Hildegard Binder Johnson's essay, "The Germans":[25]

> . . . New Ulm 'had the reputation of an orderly and pleasant place,
> where the adherents of religious confessions and freethinkers lived in
> harmony, and enforcement of rest on Sabbath and temperance were
> unknown.'[26]

But "by 1905, the original freethinking Turners were outnumbered by religious groups."[27] The advent of World War I was particularly hard on the Minnesota Germans, and it can be assumed that use of the collection by other than the Turners would have been slight from that time onward.

Geistige Abende were held most months, including one on 25 December 1875. During these evenings various topics were debated, articles or poetry read, etc. Themes included such items as readings from Gustav Struve's *Weltgeschichte* and poems of Free Thinkers. These were publications available in the library.

From statistics reported to the national headquarters from New Ulm, a definite growth in the collection was recorded from 1867 to 1920. The number of volumes logged were 200 in 1867 and 1,700 in 1920 with the peak year being 1895 with 2,000 volumes reported. Membership rose from 46 in 1867 to 122 in 1920. These figures represented 4.3 books per member in 1867 and almost 14 volumes per member in 1920. This strengthening of the collection over time indicated significant commitment to, and usage of, the collection.

The "*Protokol Buch des Bibliothek Comittees*" (1869–1876)[28] reported hours of library operation as well. On Thursday, 27 July 1871 it was resolved that the library should be "available to members every Sunday morning from 9 to 12, and Thursday evening from 8 to 10." On Tuesday, 23 January 1872 Sunday hours were extended from eight a.m. to noon and Thursday remained the same, but also included was a resolution that "books can be loaned out any evening by a member of the Library Committee." By July 25th of that same year the Library Committee made a further resolution "that on every evening of the week, as well as on Sunday mornings, a member of the Committee should be present to care for the business of the library." The number of volumes owned was only 320 in 1872, but apparently there was enough demand for them to warrant extending library hours.

The minutes of the Library Committee also referred to problems of usage. On Sunday, 2 May 1873 a resolution was enacted to impose fines of ten cents a week for books kept longer than the fourteen-day loan period if the books were not renewed. The minutes from the general meetings of the Turnverein also recorded concern about missing volumes. On Thursday, 18 February 1875 the general meeting resolved "to list out for the Verein the missing books and to request the members who still have books in their possession to report them." In the same minutes there was a resolution "not to loan out selected books which are not in good condition."

Further evidence of the support and importance of the library at New Ulm were given in the minutes in regard to a special library room and raising money for library purchases. On Friday, 9 November 1873, it was recorded that the Turnverein wished to have a specific room in its new building designated for the library. On Thursday, 18 February 1875, it was resolved "to request the Verein to give a theater production for the benefit of the library." Theater productions were very popular in this small community and well-attended. Throughout the minutes references were made to monies to be spent on binding, indicating concern for maintenance of the collection as well. All of the above references indicate that the collection was actively used.

The New Ulm Turner library was the primary library available in New Ulm until the founding of the public library there in the 1930s. The only mention of other libraries in the publication, *A Chronology of New Ulm, Minnesota: 1853–1899,*[29] was a reference to the founding of a New Ulm City Library on 10 March 1860[30] and the founding of a New Ulm Library Association on 4 March 1899.[31] The former comprised 100 volumes donated by Friedrich Kapp of New York. Apparently this was a short-lived phenomenon since it was not mentioned again. It appears likely that this collection was destroyed in an Indian massacre of 1862. No further mention of the Association appeared in the chronology. It is known that the New Ulm Public Library was not established until 1937. Several other local organizations kept small libraries at the Turner Hall. Among these were the Sons of Hermann and the Junior Pioneers. It seems reasonable to assume that the Turner library would have been a major resource at least for most of the German-speaking population, who were in the majority there for many years. Even in 1970, 41% of the population in New Ulm claimed German as their mother tongue, compared to 8.3% of Minnesotans as a whole.[32]

Use of the collection declined as the succeeding generations lost some of their German-language proficiency and the literature accumulated earlier lost some of its interest to the later members. In the 1930s the collection was offered to the emerging public library, but it was refused since the titles were mostly in German and were thought to be not relevant to the modern community. The last librarian of the collection, Gebser, complained that members did not return volumes borrowed and that most of the "better" titles were being retained by members. Kurt Bell, a life-long member of the New Ulm Turners, was asked by the women of the Turnverein to review the collection, but thinking that he was acting too slowly, the women tossed most of the items in the dumpster to make room for other activities.[33]

New Ulm, Minnesota, had Turnerism as its main foundation since the original German settlement of the Chicago Land Association (1853) was purchased by the Turner Settlers' Society in three years later. Minneapolis and St. Paul, however, were much more diversified in their settlement. Hildegard

Binder Johnson has reported that in 1870 the population of Hennepin County, including Minneapolis, was 28% German, while in the same year that of Ramsey County, including St. Paul, was 37% German.[34] In 1860, New Ulm had only two non-Germans in its entire population of 635.[35]

The following chart gives an overview of the library holdings for the Turnvereins in the Twin Cities area from the late 1860s until 1920 as reported to the national headquarters. The earliest reporting date, date of largest holdings, and last holdings reported or that given in 1920 are supplied here:

MINNEAPOLIS:

Minneapolis TV	St. Anthony TV	West Minneapolis TV
(founded 1866)	(founded 1857)	(founded 1865)
1867 40 vols.	1867 65 vols.	
1885 143 vols.	1895 150 vols.	1873 50 vols.
	1920 50 vols.	1895 210 vols.

ST. PAUL:

St. Paul TV	TV St. Paul	Germania TV	West Seite TV
(founded 1858)	(founded 1896)	(founded 1886)	(founded 1888)
(became Germania		(disbanded 1895)	(joined with TV
TV in 1886)			St. Paul, 1913)
1858 53 vols.	1900 50 vols.	1890 320 vols.	1890 0 vols.
1880 230 vols.	1920 310 vols.	1895 1200 vols.	1910 200 vols.

Some records for the St. Anthony Turnverein,[36] St. Paul Turnverein,[37] Turnverein St. Paul,[38] and the West Seite Turnverein[39] are held at the Minnesota Historical Society. Neither library holdings nor concrete records of library usage are among them. The Turnverein with the largest holdings, Germania Turnverein, lost its building and presumably its library collection to fire. The Germania Turnverein had also included the Deutscher Verein,[40] which may explain its larger library holdings. Many of the Germania Turnverein members joined the West Seite Turnverein after 1895. The Turnverein St. Paul (called the St. Paul Turners following 1940) also lost its building to fire in 1943.

St. Anthony, a suburb of Minneapolis after 1872, was a major, early German settlement in the Twin Cities area. The settlement here concentrated earlier than Minneapolis because the falls there provided the power needed for both the lumber industry and flour mills. The St. Anthony Turnverein was also developed early in this area, being founded 27 January 1857. The only mention of the office of librarian found in its minutes from 1868 to 1926[41] was in the year 1870. On 4 January 1868 there was a resolution to continue a subscription to the *Gartenlaube*. Most of the minutes dealt with social activities and *Turnen*. Because of the lack of information in the minutes and the relatively small size of the collection, it must be concluded that the library of this Turnverein was not a major concern of this organization, although it was very active socially and in Turner events. The limited statistical information on the other two Turnvereins in Minneapolis also suggests that libraries were not a high priority for these organizations.

The major library available to the Minneapolis area at this time was that of the Minneapolis Athenaeum, founded in 1860, which became the free public library in the late 1880s. The Athenaeum had been a subscription library whose directors "wished the institution to remain a place for serious and meaningful work"[42] rather than a place for reading popular works. Hlavsa reported that although Minneapolis had over 32,000 residents in 1875, only about 279 were paid subscribers to the Athenaeum.[43] *Public Libraries in the United States* reported that the Athenaeum had 292 subscribers and a yearly circulation of 6,948 in 1875.[44] By 1884, with a new board of directors and a new librarian in place, movement was initiated to have the Athenaeum become part of a new free public library for Minneapolis. The doors of a new building for the Minneapolis Public Library were opened in 1889. The new library contained 42,000 volumes on open shelves.[45] After 1895, "the library began catering more to the tastes of the public—which had always had great interest in novels."[46] It was reported that "[by] 1891 the library was second only to Boston in the percentage of its collection circulated."[47] Examination of lists of titles purchased for the library from 1897 to 1901 found in the papers of Samuel Hill[48] revealed that almost all were English-language titles with a few being in French and none in German. The Athenaeum and later Minneapolis Public Library apparently was primarily English-language oriented during this time period.

The only other libraries listed for Minneapolis in the 1875 survey of public libraries in the United States were for a theological library, two academic libraries, and a Young Men's Christian Association library of 500 volumes with a yearly circulation of 1,600. It seems likely that few of the generally anti-clerical Turner members would have made much use of any of these libraries unless perhaps they were upper-class businessmen. Much more research would have to be done to gain a clearer picture of what and how much the contemporary German settlers were reading in the Minneapolis area.

On the other hand, the St. Paul area had a higher concentration of Germans, more active Turnvereins, and the largest Turnverein library in the Twin Cities. Johnson stated that the German "activity in Minneapolis has been called 'a weak reflection' of that in St. Paul"[49] She further opined that this was probably in part due to the difference in the sizes of German populations, but also in part to the restriction of Sunday theatrical performances in Minneapolis, which continued in the 1880s. Such performances were often money-making events which helped support clubs. It should be remembered that workers usually had only Sunday as a free day to participate in such activities.

As early as 1852 a reading society was formed by the Germans in St. Paul, Der deutsche Lese- und Bildungsverein, "'for the advancement of culture, enlightenment, and freedom of thought.'"[50] This group was incorporated as the German Reading Society in 1854 with choral, dramatic, and gymnastic divisions. An 1857 catalog from the St. Paul Leseverein is preserved in the Minnesota Historical Society.[51] This catalog contained 48 titles in English, primarily United States federal documents, and 150 German-language titles. In 1858 its gymnastic section formed the St. Paul Turnverein. Thus, this was an instance in which the Turnverein developed from a reading society and presumably had access to its collection. It would appear from the statistical reports that the St. Paul Turnverein, later the Turnverein Germania, also developed its own substantial library collection. In the Minnesota Historical Society's synopsis of the archival records, written by Rudi Anders the following description is given:

> Minutes of meetings and newspaper articles of the late 1860s, 1870s and 1880s show that the Saint Paul society [St. Paul Turnverein] was very active, not only in the field of physical education and training, but also that it maintained a good library, conducted German and drawing classes, and had a Sunday school program. In addition, the society sponsored concerts and dramatic presentations.[52]

This synopsis was developed in part from information supplied by Ferdinand Uebel who gave most of these materials to the Minnesota Historical Society.[53] Uebel also stated that the Turner members were instrumental in establishing first the Freie Deutsche Schule in October 1858 and then a German-English School Society (1862), later called the German English Academy (1869). Thus, an interest in education and reading was expressed very early. Upon the destruction of the Deutscher Verein's building by fire in 1886, this group joined with the St. Paul Turnverein to become the Turnverein Germania. At this point, significant growth in the library collection took place. It might be assumed that the increase in membership assisted this endeavor. The minutes from the Deutsche Verein from 1871–1875 listed a librarian as one of the main officers of that organization, but the minutes themselves dealt primarily with social activities. A librarian was also listed as one of the principal officers of the St. Paul Turnverein in those surviving minutes from 1866 to 1870. It was also noted in the minutes of 7 January 1867 that the library would be open every Saturday from 1:30 p.m. Library reports were made regularly, but the texts of those reports were not given. Mention was made that "Schünemann-Pott" was read by members here, similar to New Ulm. Unfortunately, further minutes of the Turnverein St. Paul or its successor, Turnverein Germania, were not available. However, the size of the library collection, the administrative level of the librarian within the organization, and the frequent mention of the library or librarian in the minutes indicate that the library played a significant role in this Turnverein up to its dissolution in 1895. The dissolution of the Turnverein Germania was a result of a fire which destroyed its building as well as of the financial panic of 1893.

Although the Turnverein St. Paul (1896+) was formed much later than the St. Paul Turnverein, it also had a library. However, this library never reached the proportions of the St. Paul Turnverein. Nevertheless, a librarian was listed as one of the main officers of the administration from the start and this post continued on through all the minutes held (1934). The librarian was to oversee the administration of the library, keep an inventory of the books, and report annually in January to the membership. Mention was also made in the 15 January 1908 minutes of purchases from the Freidenker Publishing Company of Milwaukee for 50 weekly copies of *Für unsere Jugend* for the German school, and on 19 September 1927 of a subscription to the *Kölner Turnzeitung*.[54] Regular lectures were held, and programs presented were plentiful and well-attended. Many other organizations, including local high schools, used their facilities. The Damenverein also was very active.[55] Members engaged in a number of charitable activities such as working with children in hospitals and contributing to Community Chest activities. It was not until 1928 that the minutes were recorded in English. This was the same year that it was decided that instruction in gymnastic classes could also be conducted in English. This appears to have been a very active Turnverein that showed concern for its library although the collection remained modest in size. The library size may also have been a function of the increased availability of German reading material elsewhere in the community.

The minutes of the West Seite Turnverein of St. Paul[56] do not list a librarian among the officers of the club. The minutes primarily reported the approving of new members, bills for payment, and constitutional business. Reports of the

Turnschule were given, as well as information on Turner classes for a variety of age groups. The inventory records[57] of 1 January 1895 listed a bookcase worth $5.00. In 1900 this bookcase was listed as worth $10.00 while the books were given an evaluation of $3.00. In 1902 the two together were listed as $25.00, while a picture of the Verein was listed as worth $20.00. Finally, in 1912 the inventory stated that a thirty-volume *Encyclopaedia Britannica*, one index, and 87 books were owned. In comparison to the other organizations, the library did not play a significant role in the West Seite Turnverein. In 1912 this group joined the Turnverein St. Paul.

One reason for the lesser role of the library in these organizations may have been their later formation. The major impetus of the original Turners and their "radical" causes had faded somewhat by this time. The emphasis of the Turners had turned more to placing gymnastics into the public school curriculums. In addition, there appeared to have been more sources of reading material for the Germans here than was the case in Minneapolis, at least starting with the 1900s. The statistics of the St. Paul Public Library reported by William Johnson in "Notes on the St. Paul Public Library"[58] listed circulation figures for the foreign-language collection for the first time in 1899. These circulation statistics started with .94 % and rose to 3.7% in 1913, the last year presented in this historical overview. The highest circulation of foreign materials was in 1912 with 5.05%.[59]

> The circulation of foreign languages in 1913 was 18,168 or 3.7 per cent of the entire circulation, with a collection constituting 6.07 per cent of the entire collection. This was a circulation of .3 volumes per capita of citizens of foreign birth.[60]

The per capita circulation for 1910 for the entire collection was given at 1.8 volumes. The fiction collection represented 19%, or 19,240 volumes, of the collection by 1913 and was the highest circulating category at over 50%.[61] The foreign-language collection had the fifth highest ranking as far as percentage of the entire collection holdings in 1914.[62] Of these foreign-language materials, 31%, or 1,700 volumes, were German and 25% Swedish. Eighteen languages were represented, but only one volume was held for six of these.[63] The German-language holdings were by far the most numerous, reflecting the largest immigrant group. Unfortunately, the circulation figures were not further divided, but considering the collection size, it could easily be surmised that the German-language materials also accounted for a proportionately large amount of that circulation. Of the nine categories for which circulation statistics were complete in the Johnson document, that of the year 1912, foreign-language works were the fourth highest:

Category	Percentage of Circulation[64]
Fiction	51.63%
Juvenile	22.70%
Arts & Sciences	7.89%
Foreign	5.05%
Language & Literature	4.49%
Miscellaneous	2.94%
History & Biography	2.82%
Voyage & Travel	1.36%
Religion	1.12%

Clearly, the St. Paul Public Library presented a fairly well-used alternative as a source of reading material for German-language publications.

The St. Paul Public Library was not formed as such until 1882. Previous to that time it was a subscription library, the St. Paul Library Association which was formed in 1863 by the amalgamation of the Mercantile Library Association and the Young Men's Christian Association Reading Room (1856). The names of the members of early Boards of Direction indicated that it was an Anglo-dominated library. Other St. Paul libraries with over 300 volumes listed in *Public Libraries in the United States* do not appear to have been promising sources for the German-reading population in 1876. Those libraries were the Assumption School, St. Paul Home School, the Minnesota Historical Library, the Minnesota State Library, and the State Reform School.[65]

Thus, in Minnesota, the more homogeneous population of New Ulm, founded primarily by Turners, was able to build and sustain a substantial library. Its members were solid backers of Turner programs who emphasized the need for education, reading, and freethinking. The earlier St. Paul Turnverein (1858), later Turnverein Germania, also had an adequate German population to support a substantial library, and, indeed, grew out of an even earlier German reading society. Turner groups formed later in St. Paul and those in Minneapolis, with their more diverse foreign populations, seem not to have emphasized maintaining specialized libraries as the other Turners had. The later St. Paul groups also had an alternate source of German-language reading materials at a time when fewer Germans were immigrating and successive generations were using English.

St. Louis, Missouri

St. Louis, Missouri, was also a city with a large German population and many thriving Turner organizations. Olson pointed out that St. Louis was different from Cincinnati in its development since the "German element grew with the city."[66] "St. Louis contained 5,852 inhabitants in 1830 when the Germans began to arrive while Milwaukee's population stood at 1,700 in 1840 when German immigration became markedly noticeable."[67] On the other hand, Cincinnati already had a population of 24,831 in 1830 before the Germans arrived. Olson contended that the Germans were more quickly assimilated into the social structure in this growing community with its wider ethnic mix on the, then, frontier. A specific, localized German community was not identified by Olson. However, Binz countered that German sub-communities did exist in that "nationalities managed to live separated on the same street, or block-wise," even though they intermingled with other ethnic groups around a place of work.[68] Further he stated that "… we may assume that the lack of a closed German community did not prevent them from establishing ethnic neighborhoods" that were scattered throughout the city.[69] The Turner organizations were often major social centers in these communities. One can see the development of new Turner groups as the German population spread itself throughout the city. Binz has told us that, unlike many other Turner groups, the splits into new Turner organizations were because of this population shift rather than for ideological reasons. The older Turner groups often supported the newer ones.[70] See Illustration 5.1 for a distribution overview of Turner locations in St. Louis.[71] Binz has concluded that "the turnvereins' communal structures conveyed some sort of stability of existence to the turner by bridging the gap between the outward society and his individual being."[72]

Twenty-seven St. Louis Turner organizations were identified in the national Turner statistics from 1866 to 1920. The list below indicates the highest number of volumes reported for those reporting library holdings to the national during this period:

Society	Founding Date	Highest Volumes	Year Reported
St. Louis Turnverein	1850	5,000 vols.	1920
St. Louis Concordia TV	1875	2,500 vols.	1920
North St. Louis TV	1868	1,650 vols.	1920
Olympic TV	1912	1,450 vols.	1920
TV West St. Louis	1879	1,002 vols.	1910
TV Humboldt	1894	600 vols.	1905

APPENDIX III

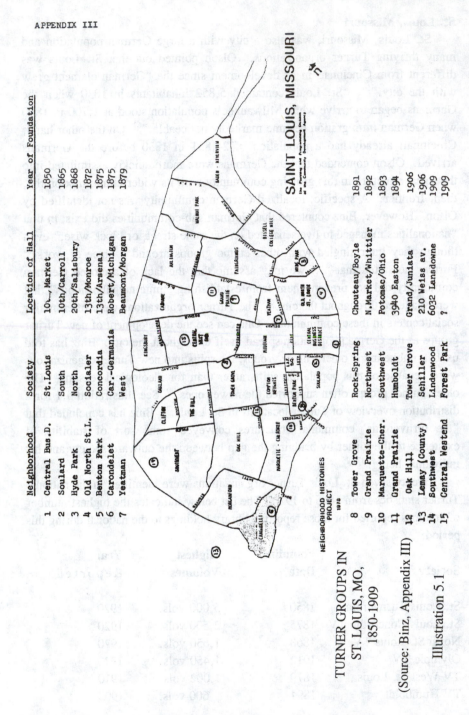

Neighborhood	Society	Location of Hall	Year of Foundation
1 Central Bus.D.	St.Louis	10.,Market	1850
2 Soulard	South	10th/Carroll	1865
3 Hyde Park	North	20th/Salisbury	1868
4 Old North St.L.	Socialer	13th/Monroe	1872
5 Benton Park	Concordia	13th/Arsenal	1875
6 Carondelet	Car.-Germania	Robert/Michigan	1875
7 Yeatman	West	Beaumont/Morgan	1879
8 Tower Grove	Rock-Spring	Chouteau/Boyle	1891
9 Grand Prairie	Northwest	N.Market/Whittier	1892
10 Marquette-Cher.	Southwest	Potomac/Ohio	1893
11 Grand Prairie	Humboldt	3940 Easton	1894
12 Oak Hill	Tower Grove	Grand/Juniata	1906
13 Lemay (County)	Schiller	210 Weiss av.	1906
14 Southwest	Lindenwood	6032 Lansdowne	1909
15 Central Westend	Forest Park	?	1909

NEIGHBORHOOD HISTORIES
PROJECT
1970

TURNER GROUPS IN
ST. LOUIS, MO,
1850-1909

(Source: Binz, Appendix III)

Illustration 5.1

Society	Founding Date	Highest Volumes	Year Reported
South St. Louis TV	1865	420 vols.	1880
TV Carondelet Germania	1875	150 vols.	1914
South West TV	1893	50 vols.	1914
Schweizer National TV	1887	12 vols.	1905
St. Louis Vorwaerts TV	?	12 vols.	1880

Sixteen of the 27 societies (59.3%) did not report any library holdings to the national organization. Of those reporting no holdings, only one was established before 1890. As can be seen above, for the most part the older societies reported larger holdings and maintained them longer. Once again, the later establishment of Turnvereins tended to correspond to the lack of emphasis on societal libraries as English became more dominant in the organizations, as the more radical nature of the Turners eased, and as other sources of German-language reading materials became more readily available.

The St. Louis Turnverein was reported in *Public Libraries in the United States* as having 2,000 volumes in 1875 of which 250 were in English. Twenty newspapers and magazines were available. It was further reported that the reading room was open only two nights during the week.[73] The yearly circulation was given as 900.[74]

St. Louis did, in fact, have other significant sources of German-language reading materials. One reason for this may have been that, as Olson charged, German-Americans assimilated relatively rapidly into the social structure of the city. Many of the German immigrants coming to St. Louis had some money for investment in land or businesses, and many were skilled workers or tradesmen, providing needed services. Olson stated that the influx of Germans largely accounted for growth and "evolution from a commercial entrepot to a commercial-industrial center."[75] Thus, it is not surprising to find here an organization such as the Deutsches Institut with an extensive library, primarily in German. Its library catalog from 1860 listed many current publications in the fields of science, art, and industry.[76] *Public Libraries in the United States* showed its holdings at 1,000 volumes in 1875.[77] This was a subscription, "research" library although it did have some classical prose fiction works. Lectures were held to supplement income for book purchases.

Likewise, German-language titles were numerous among those works offered by the Public School Library, the forerunner of the St. Louis Public Library. The Public School Library was founded through the efforts of the school superintendent, Ira Divoll, in 1865. He wanted a "library for the mass of the people, and not for the favored few," and one that "must be accessible on very low and easy terms—as nearly free as possible."[78] The School Board kept control over the library, providing duplicate collections of lighter reading throughout the community in the 1870s. Many other library collections, private and societal were actively solicited to join with the Public School Library. The St. Louis German Institute was one of these with a collection of 676 volumes.[79] Although efforts were made to keep the fee low for the Public School Library, one did have to pay the subscription fee to borrow books. By 1874, however, non-members could use the titles in the library free of charge. Among the holdings of the Public School Library in 1875, 19.3% were novels and 10.7% were juvenile literature. "The average circulation for home use [showed] 52%. of novels, 26%. of juveniles."[80] This was very similar to the St. Paul Public Library circulation figures. A classified catalog of the German works held in 1880 contained 181 pages of listings under the four major categories of "Wissenschaft," "Kunst," "Geschichte," and "Reference and Magazines."[81] The first three categories were further subdivided for the reader. The catalog was apparently produced in parts to which the reader could subscribe. One announcement referred to a price for the previous year's catalog, so it might be assumed that was a service offered regularly. Later German-language catalogs in 1898 and 1903[82] contained only German prose fiction. On the back of the 1903 catalog was listed 59 "Delivery Stations" and the scheduled delivery days. The majority of the establishments listed appear to be German-owned businesses such as pharmacies. A history of the St. Louis Public Library, *Fifty Years of Progress of the St. Louis Public Library, 1876–1926*, by Charles H. Compton stated that until 1909/10 the only foreign languages collected were German and French with the emphasis on the former.[83] "In 1877 the library had 1,518 standard works and 866 books of fiction in the German language."[84] In 1875/76 40,986 volumes were recorded for the total collection.[85] If, indeed, the same year was being discussed, the German-language material would have accounted for approximately 5.8% of the collection. Unfortunately, circulation figures for the German collection were not given in this publication. However it did mention the creation of a special committee for selection of German materials in 1884/85. By 1902/03 some 10,000 volumes in German were owned by the library.[86] The library finally became a free public library in 1898 at which time the circulation increased dramatically. It is obvious that the St. Louis Public School Library, later St. Louis Public Library, would have been an excellent resource for German-language readers who had the subscription price. The availability of this German-language collection could easily have been one reason the later Turnvereins there chose not to emphasize societal libraries.

However, as was shown above, several of the St. Louis Turnvereins did maintain substantial collections well into the 1920s. This might have been because the Turnverein was already a social center for the community and one which served the whole family. A member and his family had the right to participate in gymnastics, social, and cultural affairs of all kinds, and to use the library without additional charge. Since most probably would have become a member for social reasons, the use of the library would have been a bonus, readily accessible within the community. More recent immigrants also had the Turnverein community as a support apparatus while acclimating themselves to the new environment. The Turner groups had many mutual benefit aid programs and assisted other Turners nation-wide. Olson further stated that the "Turners were more efficiently organized than any other group of societies in the city. In 1911, the St. Louis Turnbezirk represented about 5,000 members."[87] Thus, the Turners in St. Louis commanded a significant presence. Some of their successes contributed to their own decline in later years. These successes included introducing physical education into the school curriculums, the promotion of public playgrounds, and the support of German-language instruction in the public schools. The Turner organizations were no longer the unique place for these activities.

Milwaukee, Wisconsin

Milwaukee, Wisconsin, was another significant German community in the Midwest that hosted German-American Turnvereins and their libraries. The original settlement was "predominantly a Yankee-Yorker village" according to Bayrd Still.[88] The eastern Anglo-Americans dominated the political scene for an extended period of time despite the large influx Europeans, especially Germans. "By 1850, some 64% of the city's population were of foreign birth, and of the total population more than a third was German."[89] The German community continued to grow rapidly, but the rapid integration which was described in St. Louis did not occur. Rather, according to Still, the German society existed in parallel with the Anglo, each having its full accompaniment of social provisions such as voluntary fire and military companies, relief societies, theater, press, etc.[90] Still described this situation as having continued through to 1870. In the following period from 1870 to 1910, the German-Americans garnered more political power in the city and

at the arrival of the twentieth century the processes of urbanization were welding the formerly separate German and American societies of the century before into a fundamentally American community, albeit one in which the flavor and appearance of Teutonism still remained.[91]

By 1910 only 17% of the total Milwaukee population declared themselves to be native-born Germans, but "more than half of the residents (53.5%) were still identified as of Teutonic background."[92] In 1940 more than 20% of the population still spoke German.[93] However, the process of assimilation of the German-Americans was more complete than that of later immigrants to Milwaukee. The process of assimilation was more a combining action as described by the editor of the *Milwaukee Sentinel* in 1904: "If life in the United States had Americanized the German immigrants, he wrote, that latter had 'to a perceptible and wholesome degree Germanized' the Americans."[94]

Colson stated that "not more than 5% of approximately 1,200 paid up members of the principal social library, the Young Men's Association" were German.[95] This does not seem surprising given the divided communities that existed for most of its operation from 1847 to 1877. Language would also have been a decisive factor in its use by many German-speaking residents. Colson compared this adversely with one of the music societies, founded for the most part by Germans, but which had a number of non-German members and several non-German officers during the same period. Rather than viewing this as a negative example, Still attributed the existence of many cultural institutions, including music, to German influences.[96] Music would have been one integrating element not requiring language as a primary basis, thereby bringing the two groups together.

The German community was in no way uninterested in libraries and reading. Still claimed that the combined circulation of the German press in Milwaukee in 1884 was about twice that of the English press. However, this was reversed by 1910.[97] Many German organizations had their own libraries, including the Verein Freier Maenner, established in 1853, the Germania Association, established in the early 1870s, and the various Turnvereins. The first board of the newly formed Milwaukee Public Library contained several Teutonic names such as Trumpff and Weiss. The Public Library also flourished under the mayoral Social Democratic rule supported by the German-American community.[98]

The Milwaukee Turnverein library and that of the German-English Academy were the two distinctively German-American libraries among the ten reported for Milwaukee in *Public Libraries in the United States* for 1875.[99] The German-English Academy, founded in 1853, recorded holdings of 650 volumes. This Academy was the first in Milwaukee to offer kindergarten programs.[100] The first permanent home of a Turn Teachers' Seminary for training Turner instructors was in Milwaukee, 1875–1889, 1891–1906. In 1891 a new building for the Turn Teachers' Seminary was opened. This was a joint structure with a new building for the German-American Teachers' Seminary. The latter was to supply the academic side of the training while the Turn Teachers' Seminary supplied the physical education for its students and those of the German-American Teachers' Seminary. The Turn Teachers' Seminary was held in Indianapolis from 1889 to 1891 and was finally returned permanently to Indianapolis in 1907 adopting the name Normal School.

The Turner national statistics from 1866 to 1920 listed eight Milwaukee Turner organizations, each recording library holdings. The most prominent library collection was held by the Milwaukee Turnverein founded in 1853.

Society	Founding Date	Highest Volumes	Year Reported
Turnverein Milwaukee	1853	6,400	1914
TV der Nordseite	1869	875	1880
TV der Südseite	1868	500	1905
TV Bahn Frei	1890	402	1900
TV Jahr	1895	198	1905
TV Vorwaerts	?	52	1890
TV der Ostseite	1869	40	1880
TV Humboldt	?	25	1895

As in the case of St. Louis, the largest collection, showing the most growth, and presumably use, was held by the oldest and largest Turnverein. *Public Libraries in the United States* listed its statistics for 1875 as having a collection of 1,311 volumes and a yearly circulation of 1,650 volumes.[101]

The Turnverein Milwaukee library grew from 475 volumes in 1866 to 6,400 volumes in 1914. There was substantial interest in the growth of this collection. The best comments on usage of this collection were in an article by Walter Osten in *The Milwaukee Turner* of May 1945. He wrote:

It is significant that during the gay nineties the library lost its appeal and importance for the Turners, which, however, does not mean that the Turner stopped reading entirely. On the contrary, they increased their reading, although their attitude towards German literature changed.[102]

Osten went on to say that the newer generations of German-American Turners were fluent in English. Yet there were no English-language literary volumes in the collection.

> This seems strange, but can easily be explained. The new public library was built and opened to the public in 1894. It contained an excellent collection of progressive and diversified literature, including a large German library. New current issues were added daily, while the service was incomparable. Everything was done to encourage reading. The Turners took advantage of this oportunity [sic] and thereby neglected their own library, which in time was completely forgotten.[103]

The "best" of the collection was characterized by Osten as coming during its intensive growth period previous to the Civil War.

> The titles, the authors, and the subject matters present the highlights, and the depths of mental gymnastics during the years of growth. . . . This collection is of definite 48'er origin.[104]

The Milwaukee Turnverein library was given in 1945 to the Milwaukee County Historical Society which later gave it to the Max Kade German-American Center at the University of Kansas at Lawrence where it is still housed.

Comparison of circulation with other libraries listed in *Public Libraries in the United States* is difficult since only one other library in Milwaukee reported circulation figures. The South Side Library and Literary Association with 2,500 volumes had a yearly circulation of 20,000 volumes. This was a subscription library. Unfortunately the major social subscription library listed, the Young Men's Association, which was founded in 1847 and comprised 15,000 volumes, did not give a circulation statistic. This library was later to become the nucleus of the Milwaukee Public Library established in 1878. Bayrd Still reported that "some 9,958 volumes together with numerous pamphlets and magazines"[105] were transferred to the city in 1878 after the Association fell on difficult financial times. As a public library it sustained a substantial German collection. The Milwaukee Public Library produced several catalogs of its German-language holdings of which it still preserves one for 1882 (112 pages) and one for 1910 (118 pages).[106] Also, the statements of Osten quoted earlier confirm the value of the Public Library collection, both in English and German, to the Turners.

Again, the Turners in Milwaukee warrant much more intensive research than can be given in this study. However, the information gathered here confirms the general view of Turner libraries seen in other mid-Western German-American communities. The oldest and largest Turnvereins also had the largest libraries. Those organizations formed much later, in Milwaukee's case the 1890s, had smaller libraries. All of the Turnvereins had some kind of library, however small. At the same time, additional questions are raised as to why some of the other earlier Milwaukee Turner groups did not develop larger library collections. Certainly none of these groups equalled the Turnverein Milwaukee in its membership size. The overall largest memberships for all Milwaukee Turner organizations peaked around 1895. The Turnverein Milwaukee reported 614 members in 1905 with 400 still being reported in 1920. The next highest membership was the Turnverein der Südseite with 295 members recorded in 1895 but only 190 for 1920. Thus, the second highest membership is half that of oldest Milwaukee organization by 1920. Only one other Turner organization, or the third out of eight total, even submitted statistics to the national headquarters for 1920, that of the Turnverein Bahn Frei at 182 members. Many did not survive into the twentieth century. Size of membership corresponded with larger library size in Milwaukee except in the Turnverein which was established much later in the nineteenth century.

Cincinnati, Ohio

Cincinnati is the home of one of the oldest Turnvereins in the United States, founded in 1848. However, the German-speaking population was a significant factor in this Ohio River community well before the arrival of the Forty-eighters and successive immigrant waves. Wittke noted that by 1840 Germans already made up 23% of Cincinnati's population.[107] The Turnvereins were a major contribution of the Forty-eighters and, as in other communities, became an influential social center of German-American activities. Doebbert cited Max Burgheim in stating that the Central Hall of the Turners in Cincinnati "was soon destined to become the social and political hub of the later German-American community."[108] This sentiment was also reflected by Tenner in *Cincinnati sonst und jetzt*: "Die Turnhalle ist von jeher ein Centralpunkt des freien und socialen deutschen Lebens gewesen und bildet heute noch eine feste Burg deutsch-amerikanischer Bildung."[109] Forty-four of the more prominent German-American clubs, with the exception the German Literary Club, met at the Central Turner Hall.[110] Although many of the German-speaking population who were gaining more wealth moved with others out of the city center, the Over-the-Rhine area of Cincinnati still played a social role, "keeping the physically scattering ethnic community together at least in spirit."[111] The Central Turner Hall was still located in this area before World War I. These statements show the sense of importance the Turner Halls had in the lives of Cincinnati German-Americans. However, evidence of usage of the libraries of the Turnvereins is again elusive since no loan records were located. The size and growth of the libraries, circulation as reported in 1875, as well as information in minutes are the best indicators of use available.

The statistics were reported to the national headquarters from 1863 to 1920 of four Turner societies in Cincinnati: Cincinnati Turngemeinde (1848), Nord-Cincinnati Turnverein (1881), West Cincinnati Turnverein (1881), and Lick Run Turnverein (recorded in 1885). Only the first, Cincinnati Turngemeinde, had a library of substance with the highest number of volumes listed as 5,000 for 1867, but the number had dropped to only 1,500 volumes by 1920, the last year the researcher recorded. The highest number of volumes for the others were 200 (1905), 260 (1905), and zero respectively. No volumes were listed for the library of the Nord-Cincinnati Turnverein from 1910 to 1920 even though the membership for this group was higher than any other, i.e., 900 in 1910 to 500 in 1920. In comparison, the highest membership number for the Cincinnati Turngemeinde was 560 in 1867, although by 1920 this membership had fallen to 170. Similar to other cities, the oldest Turnverein had the largest library and had maintained it longer than those forming later. Over the time period in consideration the statistics frequently fluctuated indicating that the collection was not a steady entity.

Because of several factors it is not surprising that only one Turnverein had a substantial library. Until shortly before World War I Cincinnati was almost bilingual in many of its important educational and public institutions:

> all forty-seven schools in the Cincinnati elementary and intermediate
> system maintained special classes to instruct them in German.[112]

and:

> In other contacts with the English-speaking community, provisions had
> been made which come close to recognizing officially the bilingual status
> of the city. The public library had since 1865 acquired German books,
> and the newest publications in German were available from then on.[113]

German-language materials were available for reading through a number of institutions at an early date. These included such organizations as the Young Men's Mercantile Library, which obtained its first foreign-language subscriptions to periodicals as early as 1847. The library made its membership open to all classes of citizens in 1871 and was known to have a large fiction collection.[114]

Another such institution was the Cincinnati Public Library, which contained a massive German-language collection. This library also started at a very early date for the Midwestern region. Although earlier versions of this library are claimed to have begun as far back as 1802,[115] it was not until 1867 that city taxes were regularly collected to support such an endeavor. Venable stated that in "1868 over 4,000 volumes were added to the collection," which included "a good collection of German books." He stated further that only 350 of these volumes were novels.[116] Tenner stated that the library had 98,000 volumes in 1878 of which 10,000 were books in German.[117] The 1885 *Finding List of Books in the Public Library of Cincinnati*[118] is alphabetically arranged with a separate section for fiction in various languages. Many German-language titles are represented in the main body of the *List*, and German titles occupy 53 of the 326 pages (16.3%) of prose fiction. English-language fiction comprises the largest section at 68.4% of the pages, followed by French prose at 14.7% of the pages and other languages at 0.6% of the prose fiction pages. The English-language section also included translations into English from other languages. The circulation statistics of 1874/75[119] collected in *Public Libraries in the United States* indicate that the German collection was also well used in Cincinnati. Circulation of German and French literature as a group was cited at 11.2%, higher than any other of the four out of 24 libraries reporting in this category:

Library	Percentage of Circulation German & French Literature[120]
San Francisco Mercantile Library	5.2%
Chicago Public Library	2.87%
Indianapolis Public Library	5.0%
Cincinnati Public Library	11.2%

As with other libraries the "English prose fiction and juveniles" category produced the highest circulation at 73.8%. That figure was comparable to the other libraries reported. Similar to Indianapolis, the "German and French literature" category was the second highest circulation category. However, many of the German-language materials in other disciplines were also well-used and respected. Doebbert noted a mandate by the 1918 Library Board of Trustees to remove all German books, periodicals, and newspapers from the shelves of the Public Library with the exception of those titles needed for industrial concerns and students of the sciences. The latter could be used only with special written permission.[121] By the end of October 1919 all books in German dealing with chemistry and music were returned to the shelves, and by 1921 almost all German books were again on the shelves with new purchasing resumed in 1923.[122] The community, or at least the librarian, recognized the value of information contained in the German works they had so carefully acquired. Likewise a pamphlet produced in 1886 by "A Committee of Citizens" which was critical of the contemporary administration of the Public Library, took pains to comment favorably on the Library's former administration and collection. The Citizens cited two articles praising the content of the library written by a visiting scholar. Both articles cited were from German-language newspapers, the *Cincinnati Volksfreund* and the *Illinois Staatszeitung* (Chicago).[123] This tends to reinforce the concept that the German-American community took great pride in the Public Library collection.

The early availability of this strong and well-used collection would certainly have influenced the later-forming Turnvereins. There would be little necessity to develop private society libraries when materials wanted were readily available elsewhere. The few more radical materials or more specific Turner publications could easily have been purchased and housed at the local Turner Halls without building a large general collection. Also, by the time the later Turnvereins were established in Cincinnati, the societies had become more conservative in nature.[124] Doebbert also mentioned that the central Cincinnati Turngemeinde acted more as a federation of Turner societies.[125] Since all Turner societies were open to other Turners, its central library probably would also be available to them.

The minutes of the Cincinnati Turngemeinde[126] contain some items of interest in regard to usage. These minutes indicated a separate Library Committee existed. However, separate minutes for this Library Committee were unavailable. The general minutes of the society usually recorded only that reports of the Library Committee were read and accepted. Reports on "intellectual evening" programs were also given regularly including such activities as dramatic readings and debates. Items that directly show interest in the library and its use vary. On 23 October 1858 the Building Committee read a resolution requesting that a large library and reading room be established in a new building then being planned. At a special session on 11 November 1858 resolutions were outlined on conditions for taking over the library of the Lese- und Bildungsverein. Further discussion on this matter was held on 20 November 1858. However, Körner has noted that the Deutscher Lese- und Bildungsverein, founded in 1844, dissolved its membership at the time of the Civil War, giving its 4,000-volume collection to the Männerchor singing society which supposedly held the collection until the writing of Körner's book in 1880.[127] Although the minutes outlined the conditions of the merger, Körner's statement puts in doubt if it ever actually took place or, if so, if the collections were later separated.

At a business meeting on 14 January 1860 several resolutions were passed regarding the Turner library. One required the library to be open every weekday and Sunday afternoon. A member of the Library Committee was to be in attendance for all open hours. Four specifically named newspapers from Germany were to be subscribed to for the reading room and a chess set was to be acquired. The *Committee für Geistige Ausbildung* was also charged with holding "intellectual evenings" every Wednesday to include readings and free discourse and to foster written essays among the members to maintain the purity of the German language and to foster argumentation. Evidence that the collection was actively maintained was reflected in a 23 May 1860 resolution to have the Library Committee collect valuable periodicals for binding. Likewise, on 18 May 1862 the Library Committee was requested to suggest which journals could be eliminated with least harm to the collection. Throughout the minutes various bills for library purchases or binding were presented. Specific titles of books were most frequently mentioned when they involved titles relating to such Turner publications as *Die deutsche Turnzeitung* (Leipzig) on 15 June 1865 or *Das Gesammte Turnwesen: Ein Lehrbuch für deutsche Turnlehrer* on 24 January 1866. These titles were recommended to the Library Committee or Librarian for purchase. All of these instances reflected the active concern in the maintenance of the library, particularly during the earlier years.

In 1875 the circulation figures for the Cincinnati Turngemeinde library was given in *Public Libraries in the United States*[128] as 7,800 volumes yearly circulation from a collection of 3,310 volumes. In comparison the Young Men's Christian Association reported holdings of only 1,200 volumes, but a yearly circulation of 8,000 volumes. These statistics were supplied by the libraries in question, and further study would have to be made to ascertain why the materials offered by the Y.M.C.A. library would have been so much more popular. One indication might be that the Y.M.C.A. library reported adding 100 volumes yearly whereas the Turngemeinde library reported adding only twelve. Perhaps the Turngemeinde library was not adding enough newer materials of interest to its prospective audience, leaving that to the Public Library, which was well-established by this date.

The size of the Cincinnati Turngemeinde library was indeed remarkable given the many easily available sources of German-language reading materials. It was surely the dedication of the early Turngemeinde members, many of whom were better educated Forty-Eighters, who were deeply committed to the Turner cause of a "sound mind in a sound body" that supported the maintenance of a Turner library. As in other locations, maintenance and use probably diminished as other German-language collections came into being that provided free access, as the organizations and members aged, becoming more conservative and in line with the rest of the community, and as the newer generations used German-language materials less.

Summary

Few direct evidences of usage for Turner libraries survive. However, secondary indicators of usage can provide some understanding of library use. These indicators include: 1) the growth of the collection over time, indicating interest and support of the library; 2) such library maintenance activities as book binding; 3) recorded comments in Turner minutes relating to the library such as fund-raising efforts and the need for additional space to accommodate users; 4) comments in secondary sources about usage.

The one borrowers' record which was located by the researcher was for the Wilmington Turngemeinde, Delaware. Unfortunately the period covered, from 1906 to 1932 is toward the later period of this study. Nevertheless, analysis of these records reveals some interesting facts. The usage of the Wilmington Turngemeinde library proved very similar in categories of materials use to that experienced by many contemporary public libraries, i.e., prose fiction was the most loaned category. Despite the contemporary "scorn" for the reading of novels and popular fiction by such leading German-American intellectuals as Heinzen, and the same expression of concern by various public library boards of trustees, it cannot be disputed that this category was well-used by library patrons. Since content of Turner libraries was very similar regardless of geographical location, there is no reason to surmise that usage patterns would be different at other locations. The close relationship to public library statistics indicates that Turner libraries served similar functions for this ethnic group, especially in the earlier years before many public libraries were established or before they better served the ethnic communities.

Other measures of library usage such as growth of Turner library collections varied greatly according to location although several generalizations can be made. The older, larger Turnvereins generally supported the largest and longest surviving libraries. These collections were part of a total community package for the members as the Turner Hall became the center for social, physical, and educational activities. One membership fee provided all these resources as well as a familiar, comfortable environment while the immigrants acclimated themselves to a new homeland. Turner library usage, when measured by growth, diminished when alternative free sources for German-language materials became readily available, particularly in public libraries. Scarce monetary resources would not be used for a service freely supplied elsewhere. In addition, newer generations of Turners were more comfortable reading in English and did not have need of specialized collections. The Turners were also strong advocates of general public support of institutions for the public good such as free public schools and libraries. When their needs were being met by these institutions, the necessity for parallel entities vanished.

NOTES

[1]Wilmington Turngemeinde, Library Borrowers' Record, 1906 to 1924, Wilmington Turners Lodge Collection, Research Library, Balch Institute for Ethnic Studies, Philadelphia, PA. The "Preliminary Inventory" lists contents as 1906 to 1924 but some records date to 1932.

[2]Wilmington Turngemeinde, Catalog of Library Holdings, undated, Wilmington Turners Lodge Collection, Research Library, Balch Institute for Ethnic Studies, Philadelphia, PA.

[3]Wilmington Turngemeinde, *Constitution und Nebengesetze* (Wilmington, DE: Freie Presse, 1889).

[4]Wilmington Turngemeinde, *Platform, Constitution und Nebengesetze* (Wilmington, DE: Freie Presse, 1895).

[5]See the chapter on administration of libraries and their organization for a discussion of classification methodologies.

[6]Wilmington Turngemeinde, *Constitution* (1889), 5–6.

[7]Wilmington Turngemeinde, *Platform* (1895), 33–34.

[8]Ibid.

[9]Wilmington Turngemeinde, *Constitution*, (1889), 11–12.

[10]Ibid., 15.

[11]Wilmington Turngemeinde, *Platform* (1895), 46.

[12]Ibid., 1–32.

[13]Ibid., 1.

[14]Wilmington Turngemeinde, *Constitution* (1889), 33–34.

[15]Esther Jane Carrier, *Fiction in Public Libraries, 1876–1900* (New York: Scarecrow, 1965), 28. Carrier stated that there was "little difference between the

percentage of fiction circulated in 1876 and that circulated about 1900." For most public libraries that percentage averaged about 75 per cent of the circulation for 1876 and between 70 to 80 per cent for 1902.

[16]Harmut Keil and John B. Jentz, eds., *German Workers in Chicago: A Documentary History of Working Class Culture from 1850 to World War I* (Urbana, IL: University of Illinois, 1988), 300.

[17]U.S. Bureau of Education, *Public Libraries in the United States of America: Their History, Condition, and Management: Special Report* (Washington, D.C.: GPO, 1876; reprint, Totowa, NJ: Rowman & Littlefield, 1971), 999.

[18]James M. Bergquist, "Germans and the City," in *Germans in America: Retrospect and Prospect*, ed. Randall M. Miller (Philadelphia, PA: The German Society of Pennsylvania, 1984), 46.

[19]Keil, *German Workers in Chicago*, 166.

[20]Ibid.

[21]Ibid., 164.

[22]Walter Leinert, retired faculty member of the IUPUI School of Physical Education, interview by author, Summer 1992.

[23]The Indianapolis Public Library is now the Indianapolis-Marion County Public Library. For the purposes of this paper, it will be referred to under its earlier name, that used at the time under study.

[24]Thomas V. Hull, "The Origin and Development of the Indianapolis Public Library, 1873–1899" (M.A. thesis, University of Kentucky, 1956), 30.

[25]Hildegard Binder Johnson, "The Germans," in *They Chose Minnesota: A Survey of the State's Ethnic Groups*, ed. June Drenning Holmquist (St. Paul: Minnesota Historical Society, 1981), 153–84.

[26]Ibid., 166.

[27]Ibid.

[28]New Ulm Turnverein, Library Committee, "Protokoll Buch des Bibliothek Comittees," 1869–1875, Library, Brown County Historical Museum, New Ulm, MN.

[29]Elroy E. Ubl, comp., *A Chronology of New Ulm, Minnesota: 1853–1899* (New Ulm, MN: Printed by MMI Graphics, 1978). Compiled by Ubl from the original 1899 German ed., *Chronologie der Stadt New Ulm, Minnesota* by J. H. Strasser.

[30]Ibid., 12.

[31]Ibid., 124.

[32]Johnson, 167.

[33]Kurt Bell, interview by author, March 31, 1992, New Ulm, MN, tape recording and notes. Mr. Bell, 97-years old in 1992, is considered a resident "expert" on the history of the Turners in New Ulm and attributes his longevity to his early Turner training in physical fitness.

[34]Johnson, 168.

[35]Ibid., 167.

[36]St. Anthony Turnverein, Records, 1868–1923, 1942, & undated, Minnesota Historical Society, Minneapolis, MN, 7 boxes including correspondence, financial records, various minutes, and scrapbooks.

[37]St. Paul Turnverein, MN, Records, in Turnverein St. Paul, MN, Records, Collection P1244, Vols. 11–15, Minnesota Historical Society, Minneapolis, MN.

[38]Turnverein St. Paul, MN, Records, Collection P1244, Minnesota Historical Society, Minneapolis, MN, 7 boxes, including 18 vols. correspondence, minutes, financial records, and other records of Turnverein St. Paul and related organizations.

[39]West Seite Turnverein, St. Paul, MN, Records, undated and 1890–1913, 1930–36, 1981, Collection P1243, Minnesota Historical Society, Minneapolis, MN, 4 boxes, including 2 vols., of correspondence, minutes, inventories, and financial records.

[40]Deutscher Verein, St. Paul, MN, Minutes of Meetings and Bylaws, 1871–75, in Turnverein St. Paul, Records, Collection P1244, Vol. 17, Minnesota Historical Society, Minneapolis, MN.

[41]St. Anthony Turnverein, Minutes, 1868–1926, in St. Anthony Turnverein, Records, Collection P1405, Vols. 1–10, Minnesota Historical Society, Minneapolis, MN.

[42]Larry B. Hlvasa, "A Brief History of Public Libraries in Minneapolis/St. Paul, 1849–1900: A Slide/Tape" (Masters research project, University of Minnesota, 1978), 17.

[43]Ibid., 15.

[44]*Public Libraries*, 1069.

[45]Hlavsa, 19–20.

[46]Ibid., 20.

[47]Ibid., 21.

[48]Samuel Hill, Papers, 1895–1902, Collection A .H648, Minnesota Historical Society, Minneapolis, MN. Samuel Hill had been a member of the Board of Directors of the Minneapolis Athenaeum.

[49]Johnson, 172.

[50]Ibid.

[51]St. Paul Leseverein, *"Bücher & Schriften des St. Paul Lesevereins aufgenommen den 10ten März 1857,"* in Turnverein St. Paul, MN, Records, Collection P1244, Vol. 16, Minnesota Historical Society, Minneapolis, MN.

[52]Rudi Anders, "History of the Organization," in Turnverein St. Paul, Records, Collection P1244, Minnesota Historical Society, Minneapolis, MN, page 3. This "History" includes the history of the St. Paul Turnverein, founded in 1858, which is a different Turner group than the Turnverein St. Paul, founded in 1896.

[53]Ferdinand Uebel, "History of the Turners," in Turnverein St. Paul, Records, Collection P1244, Box 3, Minneapolis Historical Society, Minneapolis, MN.

[54]Turnverein St. Paul, MN, Minutes 1906–11 and 1924–33, in Turnverein St. Paul, Records, Collection P1422, Vols. 4, 6, Minnesota Historical Society, Minneapolis, MN.

[55]Damen Verein, Turnverein St. Paul, Minutes, 1906-1935, in Turnverein St. Paul, Records, Collection P1244, Vols. 9-10, Minnesota Historical Society, Minneapolis, MN.

[56]West Seite Turnverein, St. Paul, MN, Minutes, 1900–1913, in West Seite Turnverein, Records, Collection P1243, Vol. 1, Minnesota Historical Society, Minneapolis, MN.

[57]West Seite Turnverein, Equipment Inventories, 1891–1912, in West Seite Turnverein, Records, Collection P1243, Box 3, Minnesota Historical Society, Minneapolis, MN.

[58]William Dawson Johnson, "Notes on the History of the St. Paul Public Library," 1936, Typescript, Minnesota Historical Society, Minneapolis, MN.

[59]Ibid., 28.

[60]Ibid., 27.

[61]Ibid., 20, 28.

[62]Ibid., 20–21.

[63]Ibid., 21.

[64]Ibid., 28.

[65]*Public Libraries*, 1070.

[66]Audrey L. Olson, *St. Louis Germans, 1850–1920: The Nature of an Immigrant Community and Its Relation to the Assimilation Process* American Ethnic Groups: The European Heritage (New York: Arno, 1980), 11.

[67]Ibid.

[68]Roland Binz, "Gymnastic Societies in St. Louis, 1850–1913," (Masters thesis, Washington University, St. Louis, MO, 1983), 54.

[69]Ibid., 55.

[70]Ibid., 68.

[71]Ibid., Appendix III.

[72]Ibid., 133.

[73]*Public Libraries*, 989.

[74]Ibid., 1074.

[75]Olson, 13.

[76]Deutsches Institut für Wissenschaft, Kunst und Gewerbe, *Catalog der Bibliothek des Deutschen Instituts für Wissenschaft, Kunst und Gewerbe* (St. Louis, MO: Gedruckt bei Klünder & Scholz, 1860), Special Collections, Washington University Libraries, St. Louis, MO.

[77]*Public Libraries*, 1073.

[78]Ibid., 981.

[79]Ibid., 983.

[80]Ibid., 987.

[81]St. Louis Public Library, *Klassificirter Katalog, nebst alphabetischem Register der deutschen Werke, Bibliothek der öffentlichen Schulen von St. Louis, Dec. 1880* (St. Louis, MO, 1880).

[82]St. Louis Public Library, *Class List No. 2: German Prose Fiction: 1898* (St. Louis, 1898); St. Louis Public Library, *Class List No. 2: German Prose Fiction: 1903* (St. Louis, 1903).

[83]Charles H. Compton, *Fifty Years of Progress of the St. Louis Public Library, 1876–1926* (St. Louis, MO, 1926), 33.

[84]Ibid.

[85]Ibid., 34.

[86]Ibid., 35.

[87]Olson, 142.

[88]Bayrd Still, *Milwaukee: The History of a City* (Madison: State Historical Society of Wisconsin, 1965), 70.

[89]Ibid., 72.

[90]Ibid., 251.

[91]Ibid., 259.

[92]Ibid.

[93]Ibid., 453.

[94]Ibid., 263.

[95]John C. Colson, "The Rise of the Public Library in Wisconsin: 1850–1920," in *Milestones to the Present*, ed. Harold Goldstein (Syracuse, NY: Gaylord, 1978), 185.

[96]Still, 114–20.

[97]Ibid., 264–65.

[98]Ibid., 551.

[99]*Public Libraries*, 1141.

[100]Still, 414.

[101]*Public Libraries*, 1141.

[102]Walter Osten, "The Milwaukee Turner Library," *The Milwaukee Turner* 6, no. 5 (May 1945): 8.

[103]Ibid.

[104]Ibid.

[105]Still, 381.

[106]Milwaukee Public Library, [Catalog of German Books] (Milwaukee, 1882 and 1910), R 017.1 M66k and R 018.1 M65vo.

[107]Karl Wittke, "Germans of Cincinnati," in *Festschrift for the German-American Tricentennial Jubilee, Cincinnati, 1983*, ed. Don Heinrich Tolzmann, Cincinnati Historical Society Studies in Regional and Local History, No. 2, (Cincinnati, OH: Cincinnati Historical Society, 1982), 1.

[108]Guido A. Doebbert, *The Disintegration of an Immigrant Community: The Cincinnati Germans, 1870–1920* (New York: Arno, 1980), 28.

[109]Armin Tenner, *Cincinnati sonst und jetzt: Eine Geschichte Cincinnati's und seiner verdienst-vollen Bürger deutscher Zunge* ... (Cincinnati, OH: Druck von Mecklenborg & Rosenthal, 1878), 82.

[110]Doebbert, 43.

[111]Ibid., 42.

[112]Ibid., 16.

[113]Ibid.

[114]*Public Libraries*, 903.

[115]Ibid., 898.

[116]Ibid., 911.

[117]Tenner, 76.

[118]Cincinnati Public Library, *Finding List of Books in the Public Library of Cincinnati* (Cincinnati, OH: Board of Managers; J. R. Miels, Printers, 1885), Cincinnati Historical Society.

[119]Statistics for Cincinnati are actually for 1873.

[120]*Public Libraries*, 820.

[121]Doebbert, 394.

[122]Ibid., 408–09.

[123]Committee of Concerned Citizens, *The Decline and Fall of the Public Library of Cincinnati* (Cincinnati, OH: Committee of Concerned Citizens, 1886), 7–8.

[124]Doebbert, 282.

[125]Ibid., 102–03.

[126]Cincinnati Turngemeinde, Minute Books, 1856–1936, Collection Mss fT954, Vols. 11–22, Cincinnati Historical Society.

[127]Gustav Phillip Körner, *Das Deutsche Element in den Vereinigten Staaten von Nordamerika, 1818–1848*, (Cincinnati, OH: Wilde, 1880; reprint, ed. Patricia A. Herminghouse, New York: Peter Lang, 1986), 200.

[128]*Public Libraries*, 1107.

VI

CONCLUSIONS

The American Turner organizations were founded by German-Americans who were committed to developing a strong mind in a strong body. This concept was one developed in Germany by Turners who felt that physical fitness was essential to defend their country in times of war. The German Turners were one of the primary promoters of political reform and of the failed Revolution of 1848. These German immigrants to the United States were committed to education as a means of raising one's level of prosperity and as a means of participating in a democracy as an informed citizen. Libraries were founded by the local Turner organizations to provide reading materials for their membership. As early as 1854 the national federation of American Turners encouraged the local societies to establish libraries, however small, with works on progressive reform and works of good literature. During the period of this study, 1848 to 1918, over 50% of the Turner societies accomplished this goal.

These libraries were administered by volunteer librarians or library committees elected from the membership. Duties of the caretakers were frequently considered important enough to be incorporated into the constitutions and bylaws of the Turner societies. Concern for arrangement and maintenance of the collections was evidenced by use of classification systems for larger collections and in systematic binding of volumes. Rules for library operation were very similar to those of other libraries of that time period. The hours of operation generally accommodated the needs of the users, particularly Sunday openings. Early Turners were generally anti-clerical and considered Sundays an opportunity for education as well as entertainment. Many public libraries did not have Sunday hours until the 1870s.

The proportion of subject content of Turner libraries was very similar to that of German-language public library collections. Two important differences were the existence of more radical authors in the Turner collections and the presence of works dealing with physical fitness. Subject proportions among Turner collections were also very similar, but each Turner library exhibited its unique selections among the non-literary titles. As radical political issues became less prominent in Turner organizations, public library German-language collections met the needs of Turner members, and the reasons for maintaining their own separate libraries were greatly diminished.

Few direct evidences of the usage of Turner libraries survive. The loan record of one Turner society indicated that literature was the most used category. Use statistics for public libraries from this same time period exhibit similar characteristics. Growth of collections is another measure of use. The older, larger Turnvereins generally supported the largest and longest surviving libraries. These collections were part of a total community package for the members. Turner Halls were often the center of social, physical, and educational activities for many German-Americans. One membership fee provided all these resources in a familiar, comfortable environment while the immigrants acclimated themselves to a new homeland. Growth of Turner libraries declined as free alternative sources for German-language materials became more readily available, particularly in public libraries. In addition, newer generations of Turners were not as politically radical and were more comfortable reading English. The Turners were also strong advocates of free public institutions, such as schools and libraries, which served to produce an educated citizenry. When their needs were being met by these institutions, the necessity for their own parallel entities vanished.

The study of the libraries in this segment of German-American society confirms that some immigrant groups were firm believers in the establishment of libraries as a means of self-education and cultural development. The library collections of American Turners provided German-language materials on several subjects generally not available to them from other sources. As the goals of the Turner organizations altered, and as German-language library materials became more readily available through other free sources, the interest in separate library collections diminished.

The scope of this study provides an overview of library development in one segment of the German-American community with a concentration on the Midwest. There were many American Turner societies throughout the United States that warrant closer examination. Each Turner society responded slightly differently to the development of libraries based on the resources and attitudes of the local community. Detailed local studies are needed to explore this interaction. Additional primary materials need to be identified, preserved, and made available to scholars to accomplish such studies. The work of Pumroy and Rampelmann provide the scholar with a significant place to start.[1]

To complete an understanding of the role of libraries for German-American immigrants as a whole, further research needs to examine the function of libraries in other elements of German-American societies, such as the *Freie Gemeinde*, German-American businessmen's associations, and German-American parochial institutions. Similar analyses of the role of libraries in other American ethnic groups would provide new insights into library development in America.

NOTES

[1] Eric Pumroy and Katja Rampelmann, *Research Guide to the Turner Movement in the United States* (Westport, CT: Greenwood Press, 1996).

RESOURCES

Primary Sources

The following sources refer to manuscript collections, anniversary books of various Turner organizations, library catalogs, and some Turner journals. Specific citations to collections are given primarily for material referred to in the paper. Most manuscripts are in German, especially those written before 1918, and many of the printed sources are in German *Fraktur*. The Special Collections & Archives at the University Library of Indiana University-Purdue University at Indianapolis (IUPUI) is the national repository for the American Turners. Citations are listed under American Turners for convenience since the national federation experienced a number of name changes during the period of this study. Individual Turner societies also changed the forms of their names at various times, especially in 1918 with the advent of United States participation in World War I. One form of a society's name was chosen by the author for the time period under study. The form of name was usually the one most cited by the organization itself.

A number of anniversary pamphlets for individual Turner societies are also part of this American Turner collection. In addition, the Indianapolis Socialer Turnverein, the Indianapolis Turners Damen-Verein (here Indianapolis Turn-Schwestern), and the Indianapolis South Side Turners all have materials housed in Special Collections & Archives at IUPUI. These collections also include records from the many other German-American societies with which the Turners were associated, such as the Indianapolis Freidenker Verein. The remnants of the Aurora Turnverein, Chicago, Illinois, were added to this collection in 1992 and are fully cataloged with on-line access through OCLC's WorldCat. A National Endowment for the Humanities Grant had been awarded to the Special Collections & Archives to identify and record primary sources for Turner organizations through the United States. This work, *Research Guide to the Turner Movement in the United States* (1996), by Eric Pumroy and Katja Rampelmann, is an indispensible catalog of sources for researchers and elaborates on the overview given below.

The Cincinnati Historical Society has materials from 1848 to 1948 for the Cincinnati Turngemeinde under the society's later name, Cincinnati Central Turners, MSS fT954. The library catalog for this society was in the pamphlet file. Some photographs are also available in its photograph division.

The Milwaukee County Historical Society, Milwaukee, Wisconsin, houses the records for the Milwaukee Turnverein under Turner Society Collections. These include a wide variety of printed sources as well as artifacts. The Madison Turnverein materials are held by the Wisconsin Historical Society in Madison, Wisconsin. The remnants of the Milwaukee Turnverein library are in the Max Kade Documentation & Research Centre at the University of Kansas at Lawrence.

Records for many of the Turner organizations in Minnesota are held by the Minnesota Historical Society in Minneapolis. Some of the major collections are: St. Anthony Turnverein, 1868-1928, 1942 (P1405), Turnverein St. Paul, 1868-1956 (P1244), West Seite Turnverein, St. Paul, 1890-1913, 1930-1936, 1981 (P1243). As was the case in other archives, many related societies are contained within the Turner collections. The records for New Ulm Turnverein are retained by the New Ulm Turners, but some are also available at the Brown County Historical Museum along with records of early settlers.

The Missouri Historical Society has the records from 1887-1933 of the St. Louis Turnverein, including photographs. It also has published pamphlets from various St. Louis Turner societies. The catalog of the St. Louis Turnverein can be found in the Special Collections, Washington University Libraries, St. Louis. Library catalogs and other related materials for other German-American societies are held by both the Missouri Historical Society and Washington University.

The Wilmington, Delaware, Turngemeinde records and some library remnants are now a part of the Balch Institute for Ethnic Studies Research Library in Philadelphia, Pennsylvania, under the heading of the Wilmington Turners Lodge Collection. The remaining library remnants were to be transferred from the Turner society to the University of Pennsylvania.

The remnants of the St. Lawrence Turnverein library now reside at the Max Kade Documentation and Research Centre at the University of Kansas in Lawrence.

Many of the individual Turner societies still retain their early records. At times some of these records are only available from private sources. The survey project of Pumroy and Rampelmann has helped people understand the unique value of these materials, prompting several groups to donate records to local historical repositories.

The St. Louis Public Library and the Indianapolis-Marion County Public Library were very gracious in sharing their early library catalogs with the researcher as well as providing access to historical information on their respective institutions.

American Turner Topics: Official Publication of the American Turners, 1950-
1993.

American Turners. Minutes of the National Conventions. 1854-1872. Translated by Henry W. Kumpf. Undated. Typescript; *Officialle Protokolle der Tagsatzungen der Nordamerikanischen Turnerbundes, 1874-1900.* Special Collections & Archives, IUPUI University Library, Indianapolis, IN.

──────. *Jahresberichte.* 1881-1919.

──────. Statistik, 1866-1873. Special Collections & Archives, IUPUI University Library, Indianapolis, IN.

Bell, Kurt. Interview by author. March 31, 1992. New Ulm, MN. Tape recording and notes.

Brosius, George. *Brosius Goldenes-Jubiläum, 1864-1914: Fifty Years Devoted to the Cause of Physical Culture.* Milwaukee, WI: Germania Pub. Co., 1914.

Cincinnati Public Library. *Annual Reports.* 1866/67, 1876. Cincinnati Historical Society.

──────. *Catalogue.* Cincinnati, OH: Press of Wilstach, Baldwin & Co., 1871. Cincinnati Historical Society.

──────. *Finding List of Books in the Public Library of Cincinnati.* Cincinnati, OH: Board of Managers; J. R. Mills & Co., Printers, 1885. Cincinnati Historical Society.

Cincinnati Turngemeinde. Library. *Katalog der Bibliothek der Turngemeinde in Cincinnati.* Cincinnati, OH: Gedruckt bei Friedrich Lang, 1861. Cincinnati Historical Society.

──────. *Katalog der Bibliothek der Turn-Gemeinde in Cincinnati, O.* Cincinnati, OH: Ad. Frey, 1866. Library of Congress, Washington, DC.

Cincinnati Turngemeinde. Minutes. 1856-1936. Cincinnati Historical Society.

Committee of Concerned Citizens. "The Decline and Fall of the Public Library of Cincinnati." Cincinnati, OH: Committee of Concerned Citizens, 1886. Cincinnati Historical Society.

Deutscher Literarischer Klub von Cincinnati. *Festschrift zum goldenen Jubiläum des Deutschen Literarischen Klubs von Cincinnati, 1877-1927*. Cincinnati, OH, 1927. Cincinnati Historical Society.

Deutscher Verein, St. Paul, MN. Minutes of Meetings and Bylaws. 1871-75. Vol. 17 of Turnverein St. Paul Collection (P1244). Minnesota Historical Society, Minneapolis, MN.

Deutsches Institut für Wissenschaft, Kunst und Gewerbe. *Catalog der Bibliothek des Deutschen Instituts für Wissenschaft, Kunst und Gewerbe, ... nebst Charter und Statuten, Mitglieder-Verzeichniß, u.s.w.* St. Louis, MO: Gedruckt bei Klünder & Scholz, 1860. Special Collections, Washington University Libraries, St. Louis, MO.

Der Fortschritt: Organ des Socialen Turnvereins, Jahrgang 1, Nr. 1-10 (1887-88). Indianapolis, IN. Special Collections & Archives, IUPUI University Library.

Hill, Samuel. Correspondence. 1895-1897. Samuel Hill Papers, Minnesota Historical Society. Member of Board of Directors of the Minneapolis Athenaeum.

Indiana University Libraries, Bloomington, IN. "Report on the University Libraries for the Period . . ." 1944/45-49/50. Contains statistics on the American Turners Normal College library when it was turned over to Indiana University.

Indianapolis Public Library. *Finding List of the German and French Books in the Indianapolis Public Library: Authors and Titles*. Indianapolis, IN: Carlon & Hollenbeck, Printers and Binders, 1885.

————. *Finding-List of the German and French Books in the Indianapolis Public Library: Authors and Titles*. Indianapolis, IN: Issued by the Library, 1893.

Indianapolis Socialer Turnverein. *Constitution und Nebengesetze des Sozialen Turnvereins von Indianapolis, Ind., und dessen Damen- und Zöglings-Vereins . . .* Indianapolis, IN: Druck der Tribune Pub. Co., 1897.

Indianapolis Socialer Turnverein. Minutes. 1894-1904. Special Collections & Archives, IUPUI University Library, Indianapolis, IN.

————. *Seventy-Fifth Anniversary 1851-1926.* N.p., n.d.

Indianapolis Turn-Schwestern Verein. *Statuten.* N.p., n.d. Inserted inside front cover of Account Book, Turn-Schwestern Verein, 1876-1883. Special Collections & Archives, IUPUI University Library, Indianapolis, IN.

Jahrbücher der Deutsch-Amerik. Turnerei (New York). Ed. Heinrich Metzner. 1-3, 1892-94.

Johnston, William Dawson. "Notes on the History of the St. Paul Public Library." 1936. Typescript. Minnesota Historical Society.

Louisville Turnverein, Kentucky. List of Books from the Louisville Turnverein. 1990.

Madison Turnverein. Records. Wisconsin Historical Society, Madison, WI.

Max Kade German-American Document & Research Centre, University of Kansas, Lawrence, Kansas. *Catalogue.* Lawrence, KS, 1976.

Milwaukee Turnverein. Records. Turner Society Collection, Milwaukee County Historical Society, Milwaukee, WI.

New Ulm Turnverein. *Platform und principielle Beschluesse des Nordameri-kanisches Turnerbundes, sowie Verfassung, Nebengesetze und stehende Beschluesse des New-Ulmer Turnvereins.* New Ulm, MN: Druck der New Ulm Review, 1888. In Protokolle, 1875-1904, New Ulm Turnverein, New Ulm, MN. Pasted into Protokoll Buch, at 21 Juli 1888.

————. Protokolle. 1875-1904. New Ulm Turner Hall, New Ulm, MN.

————. *Turnverein New Ulm: Ein Gedenkblatt zum Goldenen Jubiläum: 1856-1906.* Edited by *Festausschuss.* New Ulm, MN: Gedruckt von der New Ulm Pub. Co., 1906.

New Ulm Turnverein. Library Committee. "Protokoll Buch des Bibliothek Comittees." 1869-1876. Library, Brown County Historical Museum, New Ulm, MN.

Rhees, William J. *Manual of Public Libraries, Institutions, and Societies, in the United States and British Provinces of North America*. Philadelphia, PA: J. B. Lippincott, 1859; reprint, University of Illinois Graduate School of Library Science Monograph Series, no. 7. Urbana, IL, 1967.

Schnetzky, Ed and W. Grisel, librarians. "Bericht der Bibliothekare des Zöglingsvereins des Turnvereins 'Milwaukee'." 13 January 1878. Turner Collection, Milwaukee County Historical Society, Milwaukee, WI.

Schubert, R. and A. Prier, librarians. "Halbjähriger Bericht der Bibliothekare des Zöglings Vereins." 4 August 1898. Turner Collection, Milwaukee County Historical Society, Milwaukee, WI.

South Side Turnverein, Indianapolis. Minutes. 1893-1903. Special Collections & Archives, IUPUI University Library, Indianapolis, IN.

St. Anthony Turnverein. *Diamond Jubilee Anniversary, 1857-1932*. Minneapolis, MN, 1932.

St. Anthony Turnverein. Records. 1868-1928, 1942, & undated. Includes: Minutes. 1868-1926. Minnesota Historical Society, Minneapolis, MN.

St. Louis Public Library. *Class List no. 2. German Prose Fiction: 1898*. St. Louis, MO, 1898.

———. *Class List no. 2. German Prose Fiction: 1903*. St. Louis, MO, 1903.

———. *Klassificirter Katalog, nebst alphabetischem Register der deutschen Werke, Bibliothek der öffentlichen Schulen von St. Louis, Dec. 1880*. St. Louis, MO, 1880.

St. Louis Turnverein. *Katalog der Bibliothek des St. Louis Turnvereins, St. Louis, Mo*. St. Louis, MO: Aug. Wiebusch & Son Printing Co., 1895. Includes handwritten additions. Special Collections, Washington University Libraries, St. Louis, MO.

St. Louis Turnverein. Records. 1887-1933. Missouri Historical Society, St. Louis, MO.

St. Paul Leseverein. "Bücher & Schriften des St. Paul Lesevereins aufgenommen den 10ten März 1857." Vol. 16 of Turnverein St. Paul Collection (P1244). Minnesota Historical Society, Minneapolis, MN.

St. Paul Library Association. *Catalogue*. Pages 1-16. St. Paul, MN: Printed by David Ramaley, 1864. Minnesota Historical Society, Minneapolis, MN.

St. Paul Turnverein. Minutes. 1866-1883. Minnesota Historical Society, Minneapolis, MN.

Turner Leben 1, no. 1-12 (Nov. 1914-Oct. 1915). North Cincinnati Turnverein. Library, Cincinnati Historical Society.

Turnverein Fortschritt (Chicago, IL). "Protokoll Buch." 8 October 1884 – 18 April 1888. Property of Elgin Turners, Elgin, IL.

Turnverein Frischauf (Aurora, IL). "Protokolle." 14 February 1907 – 20, October 1927. Property of Elgin Turners, Elgin, IL.

Turnverein St. Paul. Minutes. 1897-1933. Includes Ferdinand Uebel's "History of the Turners [in Minneapolis and St. Paul]." Minnesota Historical Society, Minneapolis, MN.

Uebel, Ferdinand & Family. Diary, Correspondence and Miscellaneous Papers. 1899-1951. Minnesota Historical Society, Minneapolis, MN.

U.S. Bureau of Education. *Public Libraries in the United States of America: Their History, Condition, and Management: Special Report*. Washington, DC: GPO, 1876; reprint, Totowa, NJ: Rowman & Littlefield, 1971.

West Seite Turnverein, St. Paul. Records. Undated and 1890-1913, 1930-36, 1981. Minnesota Historical Society, Minneapolis, MN.

Wilmington Turngemeinde. Catalog of Library Holdings. Undated. Wilmington Turners Lodge Collection, Research Library, Balch Institute for Ethnic Studies, Philadelphia, PA.

Wilmington Turngemeinde. *Constitution und Nebengesetze*. Wilmington, DE: Freie Presse, 1889.

———. Library Borrowers Record, 1906 to 1924. Wilmington Turners Lodge Collection, Research Library, Balch Institute for Ethnic Studies, Philadelphia, PA.

———. List of Titles Found at the Wilmington Turners Lodge. Comp. Monique Bourque, Archivist, Balch Institute for Ethnic Studies, Philadelphia, PA.

———. *Platform, Constitution und Nebengesetze*. Wilmington, DE: Freie Presse, 1895.

Secondary Sources

Adams, Willi Paul. *The German-Americans: An Ethnic Experience*. Am. ed., trans. and adapted by LaVern J. Rippley and Eberhard Reichmann. Indianapolis, IN: Max Kade German-American Center, Indiana University-Purdue University at Indianapolis, 1993.

Arndt, Karl J. R., and May E. Olson. *The German Language Press of the Americas (Die deutschsprachige Presse der Amerikas)*. 3d, rev. ed., and enlarged. 3 vols. Munich: Verlag Dokumentation, 1976-1980.

Bachman, Irma. "Social Conditions in Indianapolis Before 1850." Ph.D. diss., Columbia University, 1933.

Bailey, V. D. "The Germans in Indiana, with Economic Emphasis." Unpublished A.M. thesis, Indiana University, 1946

Barney, Robert Knight. "The German-American Turnverein Movement: Its Historiography." In *Turnen und Sport: The Cross-Cultural Exchange*, ed. Roland Naul, 3-19. Münster, New York: Waxmann, 1991.

———. "German Turners in American Domestic Crisis." *Stadion* 4 (1978): 344-57.

Bergquist, James H. "Germans and the City." In *Germans in America: Retrospect and Prospect*, ed. Randall M. Miller, 37-56. Philadelphia, PA: German Society of Pennsylvania, 1984.

Binz, Roland. "Gymnastic Societies in St. Louis, 1850-1913." Masters thesis, Washington University, St. Louis, MO, 1983.

Brancaforte, Charlotte L., ed. *The German Forty-Eighters in the United States*. German Life and Civilization, vol. 1. New York: Peter Lang, 1989.

Bruce, William George. "Old Milwaukee." *American-German Review* 10, no. 4 (1944): 1-14; 10, no. 5 (1944): 27-29.

Buchheim, Karl. *Deutsche Kultur zwischen 1830 und 1870*. Handbuch der Kulturgeschichte, 1. Abteilung: Zeitalter deutscher Kultur. Frankfurt am Main: Akademische Verlagsgesellschaft Athenaion, 1966.

Busse, Gisela von. *Libraries in the Federal Republic of Germany*. 2d, fully rev. and enlarged ed. by Horst Ernestus and Engelbert Plassmann. Translated by John S. Andrews. Wiesbaden: Otto Harrassowitz, 1983.

Buzas, Ladislaus. *German Library History, 800-1945*. Translated by William D. Boyd. Jefferson, NC: McFarland, 1986.

Cannons, H. G. T. *Bibliography of Library Economy*. Reprint of the 1927 ed. New York: B. Franklin, 1970.

Carrier, Esther Jane. *Fiction in Public Libraries, 1876-1900*. New York: Scarecrow, 1965.

Cazden, Robert E. "Libraries in the German-American Community and the Rise of the Public Library Movement." In *Milestones to the Present*, ed. Harold Goldstein, 193-211. Syracuse, NY: Gaylord, 1978.

———. *A Social History of the German Book Trade in America to the Civil War*. Studies in German Literature, Linguistics, and Culture, vol. 1. Columbia, SC: Camden House, 1984.

Colson, John C. "The Rise of the Public Library in Wisconsin: 1850-1920." In *Milestones to the Present*, ed. Harold Goldstein, 184-92. Syracuse, NY: Gaylord, 1978.

Compton, Charles H. *Fifty Years of Progress of the St. Louis Public Library, 1876-1926*. St. Louis, MO, 1926.

Constantine, J. Robert. *The Role of Libraries in the Cultural History of Indiana*. Indiana Library Studies, Report no. 2. Bloomington, IN, 1970.

Conzen, Kathleen Neils. "Germans." In *Harvard Encyclopedia of American Ethnic Groups*, ed. Stephan Thernstrom, 405-25. Cambridge, MA: Harvard University Press, 1980.

Davis, Donald G. "The Rise of the Public Library in Texas." In *Milestones to the Present*, ed. Harold Goldstein, 166-183. Syracuse, NY: Gaylord, 1978.

Degina, Christina, and Christiana Harzig, eds. *Deutschland im Gepäck*. Bremerhaven: Wirtschaftsverlag NW, 1987.

Deutscher Literarischer Klub von Cincinnati. *Festschrift zum goldenen Jubiläum des Deutschen Literarischen Klubs von Cincinnati, 1877-1927*. Cincinnati, OH: N.p., 1927. Cincinnati Historical Society.

Dinnerstein, Leonard, and David M. Reimers. *Ethnic Americans: A History of Immigration and Assimilation*. New York: Dodd, Mead, 1975.

Doebbert, Guido Andre. *The Disintegration of an Immigrant Community: The Cincinnati Germans, 1870-1920*. New York: Arno Press, 1980.

Dolmetsch, Christopher L. *The German Press of the Shenandoah Valley*. Studies in German Literature, Linguistics, and Culture, vol. 4. Columbia, SC: Camden House, 1984.

Downey, Lawrence J. *A Live Thing in the Whole Town: The History of the Indianapolis-Marion County Public Library, 1873-1990*. Indianapolis, IN: Indianapolis-Marion County Public Library Foundation, 1991.

Draegert, Eva. "Indianapolis: The Culture of an Inland City." Ph.D. diss., Indiana University, 1952.

Dunn, Jacob P. *Greater Indianapolis*. Chicago: Lewis Publishing Co., 1910.

———. *Indiana and Indianans*. Chicago, IL: The American Historical Society, 1919.

Faust, Albert Bernhardt. *The German Element in the United States with Special Reference to its Political, Moral, Social, and Education Influence*. 2 vols. Boston: Houghton Mifflin, 1909.

Fritsch, William. *German Settlers and German Settlements in Indiana*. Evansville, IN, 1915.

Glasrud, Clarence A., ed. *A Heritage Fulfilled: German-Americans (Die Erfüllte Herkunft)*. Moorhead, MN: Corcordia College, 1984.

Goldstein, Harold, ed. *Milestones to the Present: Papers from the Library History Seminar V*. Syracuse, NY: Gaylord, 1978.

Gradenwitz, Peter. "Books and Reading in Germany 200 Years Ago." *AB Bookman's Weekly* 8, no. 10 (7 Sept. 1987): 797-99.

Gray, Wendy. "The Origin and Evolution of the German-Canadian Turnverein Movement: A Study of Waterloo County, Canada West, 1855-1875." M.A. thesis, University of Western Ontario, 1990.

Hagen, Victor Wolfgang von. *The Germanic People in America*. Norman, OK: Univ. of Oklahoma Press, 1976.

Hawgood, John Arkas. *The Tragedy of German-America*. New York: G. P. Putnam, 1940; reprint, New York: Arno Press & The New York Times, 1970.

Helbich, Wolfgang, Walter D. Kamphoefner, and Ulrike Sommer, eds. *Briefe aus Amerika: Deutsche Auswanderer schreiben aus der Neuen Welt, 1830-1930*. Munich: C. H. Beck, 1988.

Hense-Jensen, Wilhelm. *Wisconsin's Deutsch-Amerikaner bis zum Schluß des neunzehten Jahrhunderts*. 2 vols. Milwaukee, WI: Im Verlage der Deutschen Gesellschaft, Der Germania, 1900-02.

Herminghouse, Patricia. "Women and the Literary Enterprise in Nineteenth-Century Germany." In *German Women in the Eighteenth and Nineteenth Centuries: A Social and Literary History*, ed. Ruth-Ellen B. Joeres and Mary Jo Maynes, 78-93. Bloomington, IN: Indiana University Press, 1986.

Hlavsa, Larry B. "A Brief History of Public Libraries in Minneapolis/St. Paul, 1849-1900: A Slide/Tape." Masters research project, University of Minnesota, 1978.

Hofmann, Annette R. "Bahn Frei: Das deutsch-amerikanische Turnen von seinen Anfängen bis Ende des Bürgerkrieges." M.A. thesis, Eberhard-Karls-Universität Tübingen, Germany, 1993.

Hoyt, Giles R. "Germans." In *Peopling Indiana: The Ethnic Experience*, ed. Robert M. Taylor and Connie A. McBirney, 146-81. Indianapolis, IN: Indiana Historical Society, 1996.

————. "Indianapolis: Ethnic Crossroad?" *Circular, Marion County/Indianapolis Historical Society* 9, no. 1-2 (June & Dec. 1988): 1-2; 2-4.

Holmquist, June Drenning, ed. *They Chose Minnesota: A Survey of the State's Ethnic Groups*. St. Paul, MN: Minnesota Historical Society Press, 1981.

Hull, Thomas V. "The Origin and Development of the Indianapolis Public Library, 1873-1899." M.A. thesis, University of Kentucky, Lexington, 1956.

Hyde, William, and Howard L. Conard, eds. *Encyclopedia of the History of St. Louis*. 4 vols. New York: Southern History Co., 1899. S. v. "Turners."

Johnson, Hildegard Binder. "The Germans." In *They Chose Minnesota: A Survey of the State's Ethnic Groups*, ed. by June Drenning Holmquist, 153-84. St. Paul, MN: Minnesota Historical Society, 1981.

Kaser, David. *Books and Libraries in Camp and Battle: The Civil War Experience.* Contributions in Librarianship and Information Science, no. 48. Westport, CT: Greenwood Press, 1984.

————. *A Book for a Sixpence: The Circulating Library in America.* Pittsburgh, PA: Beta Phi Mu, 1980.

Kattner, Lauren Ann. "Perpetuating German Ideas: Education and Literature in New Braunfels, Texas." Typescript from author. Garland, TX, 1987.

Keil, Harmut, ed. *German Workers' Culture in the United States, 1850 to 1920.* Washington, DC: Smithsonian Institution Press, 1988.

Keil, Harmut, and John B. Jentz, eds. *German Workers in Chicago: A Documentary History of Working-Class Culture from 1850 to World War I.* Urbana, IL: University of Illinois Press, 1988.

Keller, J. *Festschrift zur Feier des goldenen Jubiläums des Indianapolis Männerchor am 23., 24. und 25. Juni 1904.* Indianapolis, IN: Gutenberg Co., 1904.

Kershner, Frederick D. "A Social and Cultural History of Indianapolis 1861-1914." A.B. thesis, University of Wisconsin, 1950.

Knoche, Carl Heinz. *The German Immigrant Press in Milwaukee.* American Ethnic Groups: The European Heritage. New York: Arno Press, 1980.

Kolb, E. J. "Influence of the German Element in Indiana." A.B. thesis, Indiana University, 1917.

Körner, Gustav Phillip. *Das Deutsche Element in den Vereinigten Staaten von Nordamerika, 1818-1848.* Cincinnati, OH: Wilde, 1880; reprint, ed. by Patricia A. Herminghouse, New York: Peter Lang, 1986.

Kraus, Joe W. "Libraries of the Young Men's Christian Associations in the Nineteenth Century." *Journal of Library History* 10 (1975): 3-21.

Lich, Glen E. *The German Texans.* San Antonio, TX: University of Texas, Institute of Texan Cultures, 1981.

McClelland, Charles E. *State, Society, and University in Germany, 1700-1914*. Cambridge; New York: Cambridge University Press, 1980.

McMullen, Haynes. "The Founding of Social and Public Libraries in Ohio, Indiana, and Illinois Through 1850." *University of Illinois Library School Occasional Papers*, no. 51 (March 1958).

————. "The Prevalence of Libraries in the Middle West and Far West before 1876." *Libraries & Culture* 26 (Spring 1991): 441-63.

Metzner, Henry. *A Brief History of the American Turnerbund*. Rev. ed. Translated by Theodore Stempfel. Pittsburgh, PA: National Executive Committee of the American Turnerbund, 1924.

————. *History of the American Turners*. 4th rev. ed. Louisville, KY: National Council of the American Turners, 1989.

Meyer, Williams R. *History of the Turnverein Vorwaerts (Forward Turners) of Chicago, Illinois: July 24, 1867-February 12, 1956*. N.p., 1991?

Miller, C. Eugene, and Forrest F. Steinlage. *Der Turner Soldat: A Turner Soldier in the Civil War; Germany to Antietam*. Louisville, KY: Calmar Publications, 1988.

Miller, John. *Indiana Newspaper Bibliography*. Indianapolis, IN: Indiana Historical Society, 1982.

Miller, Randall M., ed. *Germans in America: Retrospect and Prospect*. Philadelphia, PA: German Society of Pennsylvania, 1984.

Moltmann, Günther. *Deutsche Amerikaauswanderung im 19. Jahrhundert: Sozialgeschichtliche Beiträge*. Stuttgart: J. B. Metzler, 1976.

Morton, Oliver P. *Die Auswanderung nach den Vereinigten Staaten von Nord-Amerika: Indiana eine passende Heimstätte für Emigranten*. Translated by C. J. Beleke. Indianapolis, IN: Joseph J. Bingham, Staatsdrucker, 1864.

Olson, Audrey L. *St. Louis Germans, 1850-1920: The Nature of an Immigrant Community and Its Relation to the Assimilation Process*. American Ethnic Groups: The European Heritage. New York: Arno Press, 1980.

Osten, Walter. "The Milwaukee Turner Library." *The Milwaukee Turner* 6, no. 5 (May 1945): 1, 8.

————. "Turner Library Favors Early American History." *The Milwaukee Turner* 6, no. 7 (July 1945): 1, 4.

Petry, Eduard. "New Ulm, Minnesota Turnverein, 1856-1906." Ed. Fredric R. Steinhauser. Translated by Auguste G. Kent. N.p., 1979. Original 1906 ed. in German. Brown County Historical Society, New Ulm, MN.

Pochmann, Henry August. *German Culture in America: Philosophical and Literary Influences, 1600-1900*. Madison, WI: University of Wisconsin Press, 1961.

Probst, George T. "The Germans in Indianapolis, 1850-1914." M.A. thesis, Indiana University, 1951.

————. *The Germans in Indianapolis, 1840-1918*. Rev. and illustrated ed. by Eberhard Reichmann. Indianapolis, IN: German-American Center & Indiana German Heritage Society, 1989.

Pumroy, Eric, and Katja Rampelmann, comps. *Research Guide to the Turner Movement in the United States*. Bibliographies and Indexes in American History, no. 33. Westport, CT: Greenwood Press, 1996.

Rampelmann, Katja. "Small Town Germans: The Germans of Lawrence, Kansas, from 1854 to 1918." M.A. thesis, University of Kansas, Lawrence, 1993.

Reinhardt, Kurt F. *Germany: 2000 Years*. Vol. 2, *The Second Empire and the Weimar Republic*. New York: Ungar, 1961.

Rinsch, Emil. *The History of the Normal College of the American Gymnastic Union of Indiana University, 1866-1966*. Indianapolis, 1966.

Rippley, LaVern J. *The German-Americans*. Lanham, MD: University of America, 1976.

Rippley, LaVern J. "Germans." In *Dictionary of American Immigration History*, ed. by Francesco Cordasco, 241-47. Metuchen, NJ: Scarecrow Press, 1990.

Rühl, Hugo. *Entwicklungsgeschichte des Turnens*. Leipzig: P. Eberhardt, 1912.

Scharf, J. Thomas. *History of Saint Louis City and County, From the Earliest Periods to the Present Day: Including Biographical Sketches of Representative Men*. Vol. 2, pp. 1770-1774. Philadelphia: Louis H. Everts, 1883. Essays on eight different *Turnvereine*.

Stein, Theodore. *Our Old School: Historical Sketch of the German-English Independent School of Indianapolis*. Indianapolis, 1913.

Stempfel, Theodore. *Fünfzig Jahre unermüdlichen deutschen Strebens in Indianapolis*. Indianapolis, IN: Pitts & Smith, 1898.

————. *Fünfzig Jahre unermüdlichen deutschen Strebens in Indianapolis*. German/English ed. Edited by Giles R. Hoyt et. al. Indianapolis, IN: German American Center & Indiana German Heritage Society, 1991.

Still, Bayrd. *Milwaukee: The History of a City*. Madison, WI: State Historical Society of Wisconsin, 1965.

Tafel, Karl, Mrs. "Early Cincinnati and the Turners." Ed. by Leonard Koester. *Bulletin of the Historical and Philosophical Society of Ohio* 7 (1949): 18-22.

Tenner, Armin. *Cincinnati sonst und jetzt. Eine Geschichte Cincinnati's und seiner verdienst-vollen Bürger deutscher Zunge, mit biographischen Skizzen und Portrait Illustrationen*. Cincinnati, OH: Druck von Mecklenborg & Rosenthal, 1878.

Thornbrough, Emma Lou. *Indiana in the Civil War Era, 1850-1880*. Indianapolis, IN: Indiana Historical Bureau, 1965.

Tolzmann, Don Heinrich. *Catalog of the German-Americana Collection, University of Cincinnati*. 2 vols. Munich: K. G. Sauer, 1990.

————, ed. *Festschrift for the German-American Tricentennial Jubilee: Cincinnati, 1983*. The Cincinnati Historical Society Studies in Regional and Local History, no. 2. Cincinnati, OH: Cincinnati Historical Society, 1982.

————. *German-American Literature*. Metuchen, NJ: Scarecrow Press, 1977.

Treitschke, Heinrich von. *History of Germany in the Nineteenth Century*. Selections from the trans. of Eden and Cedar Paul. Edited and with an introduction by Gordon A. Craig. Chicago, IL: University of Chicago Press, 1974.

Trommler, Frank, and Joseph McVeigh, eds. *American and the Germans: An Assessment of a Three-Hundred-Year History*. 2 vols. Philadelphia, PA: University of Pennsylvania Press, 1985.

Ubl, Elroy E., comp. *A Chronology of New Ulm, Minnesota: 1853-1899*. Compiled by Ubl from the original 1899 German ed., *Chronologie der Stadt New Ulm, Minnesota* by J. H. Strasser. New Ulm, MN: Printed by MMI Graphics, 1978.

————. *Historical Notes: A Glimpse at New Ulm's Past*. 2 vols. New Ulm, MN, 1982-83.

Ueberhorst, Horst. *Turner unterm Sternenbanner: Der Kampf der deutsch-amerkanischen Turner für Einheit, Freiheit und soziale Gerechtigkeit 1848 bis 1918*. Munich: Heinz Moos Verlag, 1978.

Vonnegut, Clemens. *A Proposed Guide for Instruction in Morals From the Standpoint of a Freethinker for Adult Persons, Offered by a Dilettante*. Indianapolis, IN: Hollenbeck Press, 1900; repr., 1987.

Vonnegut, Theodore F. "Indianapolis Booksellers and Their Literary Background, 1822-1860." M.A. thesis, Indiana University, 1926. Also in published form: Greenfield, IN: W. Mitchell, 1926.

Waldo, Michael J. "A Comparative Analysis of Nineteenth-Century Academic and Literary Society Library Collections in the Midwest." Ph.D. diss., Indiana University, 1985.

Wild, Robert. "Chapters in the History of the Turners." *Wisconsin Magazine of History* 9 (Dec. 1925): 123-33.

Wittke, Carl. *The German Language Press in America*. Lexington, KY: University of Kentucky Press, 1957.

————. "The Germans of Cincinnati." In *Festschrift for the German-American Tricentennial Jubilee: Cincinnati, 1983*, ed. by Don Heinrich Tolzmann, 1-9. Cincinnati, OH: Cincinnati Historical Society, 1982.

Wittke, Carl. *Refugees of Revolution: The German Forty-Eighters in America.* Philadelphia, PA: University of Pennsylvania Press, 1952.

Zeitlin, Richard H. *Germans in Wisconsin.* Madison, WI: State Historical Society of Wisconsin, 1977.

Index

New German-American Studies
Neue Deutsch-Amerikanische Studien

This series features scholarly monographs, published in German or English, that deal with topics in the humanities or social sciences pertaining to the German-American experience.

Original monographs in the following areas are welcome: history, literature, language, politics, philosophy, religion, education, geography, art and architecture, music and musical life, the theater, and contemporary issues of general interest.

All inquiries should be directed to the Editor of the series. Manuscripts should be between two and four hundred pages in length and prepared in accordance with the Chicago Manual of Style.

For additional information, contact the editor:

Dr. Don Heinrich Tolzmann
Blegen Library
University of Cincinnati
PO Box 210113
Cincinnati, OH 45221